RADICAL JOY

Christ's Call to Purposeful, Joy-filled Motherhood

Kayla Gahagan

For Elijah, Brooke, Jonah and Hannah

*You are the four greatest miracles in my life. May
you know Jesus deeply and truly, and through that,
experience your own radical joy.*

For Adam

*The best is behind us, but also before us. Thank you for
doing this with me. I love you.*

CONTENTS

INTRODUCTION

Motherhood.

They warn you: don't blink, or you'll miss it. It's a gift, it's good, and then it's gone. What they don't always tell you is that there's more, so much more, to this calling than simply keeping our eyes open.

I have come to believe that motherhood is not something to be feared or idolized, but met each day with a confident expectation that something wonderful is unfolding before us. I believe that amidst the complicated nuances of parenting, we are called to a simple, profound mission that is often overlooked: *mothering with joy.*

Whatever season of motherhood you are in, this book is for you. Amid the highs and lows and all the in-betweens of your parenting journey, I hope it reminds you of the importance of caring for your soul. Before you can truly steward the little souls entrusted to your care, you must plant yourself deeply and surely in something bigger than the here and now. It is only when we are refreshed at Christ's overflowing well, dismantling the distractions and allowing Him to gently rebuild us, that we can cease operating out of fear and instead choose to parent with insatiable joy. This is not something we can do alone. I want us to be a generation of mothers who, together, rise with joy—confident in who we are in Christ—so that we can genuinely encourage our children on their own journeys.

I am convinced of many things, not the least that friendship is like oxygen, that mothers are called to more than busyness, and that we really could make do with less. Being convinced of something, however, does not make that conviction a fact, nor relevant to every situation.

This book, then, is written with a spirit of humility. I share both my testimony and my unfiltered experiences of motherhood with the hope that we will be a generation of mothers, linking arms and being continually transformed by the presence of Jesus.

This is my prayer for you, dear reader—that you boldly claim one of the greatest gifts you have been given. Mothers, do not miss out on the joy.

Much love,
Kayla

CHAPTER ONE

UNDERWATER

The minutes before my daughter almost drowns seem ordinary—
my two kids are in the tub, the bath water sudsy and lavender-
scented, my back sticky with warmth.

It's her first birthday, and Brooke is teetering on the verge of
walking. I perch on the edge of the tub, content to watch my three-
year-old son scoop piles of bubbles onto his sister's arms. I check
my phone, my attention drawn to the time. *I could squeeze in one
more load of dishes before we leave for our friend's house.* I tell Elijah I
will be right back, and dart down the hallway to the kitchen where
I begin sliding plates into the lower rungs of the dishwasher.

I don't recall how long I was away—it couldn't have been more than
a couple of minutes. So when I hear Elijah yell out, "Mommy!",
I'm not alarmed. There is no indication that this is any different
from the hundreds of other times he has called out to me to look
at a caterpillar, or watch him tie his shoe, or play another round
of 'Go Fish'.

Over the sound of his voice, I hear the splashing of water. With a sigh, I start toward the bathroom. *Elijah must have figured out the faucet and pulled the lever to start the shower.*

But I'm wrong.

Suddenly, I find myself running. Brooke is on her back, her face underwater in the deeper end of the tub—just an inch submerged, but enough. She looks like a tiny bird in mid-flight, her blue eyes wide and terrified, her arms flapping wildly at her side, splashing the water but doing nothing to get her upright. No sound comes from her mouth. Not a cry. Not a scream. Nothing.

~

The world grows heavy and lethargic in emergencies; it gets fuzzy at the edges. It's as though our brains and hearts perform on overdrive, struggling to catalog each movement and process every action. Maybe our minds already know they will be forced to walk back through every detail, reliving the small windows of opportunity when we could have made a different decision. Perhaps, it's the foretelling of regret.

In the bathroom that day, all I could hear was the blood pounding in my ears. My skin felt electric with panic and adrenaline. It was as though my muscles and brain were at an impasse—I couldn't get to her fast enough. Tucking my hands under her armpits, I finally snatched her from the water, slapping my hand on her wet back over and over and over.

Please just take a breath.

Eventually she threw up all over the bathroom floor, and her coughs subsided into long, hard cries. Clutching my daughter's naked body tightly in my arms, my hands shook so hard I worried I might drop her.

Would I ever be able to let her go?

Later I would spend time pouring over stories of child drownings, reading gut-wrenching reports of what they call the 'silent death'. One mother described having an outdoor lunch with a girlfriend when her toddler slipped out of her sight and into the swimming pool just yards away. When they pulled his limp body from the water he was still clutching a piece of the Oreo he had just shared with his mom.

~

Brooke is now a lanky, free-spirited ten-year-old. She's a creator, a reader, my child with the inquisitive mind and overflowing imagination. I call her "my butterfly" because she floats from project to project, leaving handicrafts and love notes all around the house.

I think about how her life was almost snuffed out so early, how one careless mistake could have changed the entire trajectory of our story in just a few moments. It's that kind of deep-seated fear, the sober realization that just one lapse in judgment could take the life of your own child, that kept me up at night those first few months. Their lives—every single one of our lives, in fact—is frail, but a breath.

As mothers, some days seem to stretch on and on, the exhausting ones seeming to demand a deeper level of fortitude than any other area of my life. Yet the truth is that time is cruelly fleeting. I careened through those early years of parenthood at full-speed—optimistic, confident, wholly certain I had a grip on what I was doing. This close call, however, felt like a pivot, a fork in the road. It sobered me, it righted me, it awakened something in me regarding the brevity of our parenting years.

After pulling Brooke from the bathtub I paced the hardwood floors of our hallway, back and forth, back and forth. When my husband finally came home I handed our daughter to him, my hands trembling, my voice cracking under the weight of the lump in my throat. I waited to cry until I was alone in the shower, guilt settling on my mind like a suffocating blanket.

That night my husband and I took Brooke to our pediatrician as a precaution. The doctor looked at us with kind eyes. She pressed the metal stethoscope against Brooke's back and listened for water in her lungs, but heard only the steady flare of her heart. I waited for a lecture on drownings, something with statistics perhaps, maybe even a side comment or two. *Don't you know you should never leave a baby in a bathtub? That's parenting 101 . . . along with double checking the car seat and holding their hand when they cross the street. And yes, they can drown in the bathtub, no matter how deep the water.*

Instead, she spoke gently. Maybe she heard the shame in my voice or noticed the number of times I pulled Brooke onto my lap, rested my chin on her head, and placed my hand on her chest, feeling the warmth of her baby skin through her shirt. Holding my gaze, the pediatrician patted my arm and reminded me that accidents happen. We were to keep watch through the night, and Brooke was going to be fine. But as for me, it was too late; the fear had already taken residence in my heart.

~

Motherhood is a season of touch. No one told me how physical parenthood is, especially in the early years when your body is but an extension of theirs—breastfeeding, combing fingers through hair, hugging sweaty bodies at the beach, smearing on sunscreen and lotion, folding them into your lap to cradle a bloody knee, their sticky fingers pressed into yours, their hot breath on your cheek as they whisper in your ear.

For years I carried babies up and down the hallway as they oscillated between sleep and wails. Despite the ache stretching from my forearms, radiating through my back and up my neck, I held the cadence like a soldier in my own home: step, sway, dip, step, sway, dip . . . until I was finally met with sleepy silence accompanied only by the quiet shuffle of my feet along the carpet.

I fell into bed every night having been kissed, slobbered, hugged, crawled on, puked on, jumped on. My hair had been pulled, my legs clung to.

It's this physical interaction that extends from endless minutes into hours and days, eventually bleeding into years, that I now see embodies the role once held by the umbilical cord that bonded them to me in the womb. In the constant pumping of life and love between your heart and theirs, you become attached—two hearts inextricably linked far beyond the boundaries of birth.

They told me long ago, when my oldest was still growing inside me, that when you have children it feels like your heart exists outside your body. Your heart, they gently warned me, would forever be walking around—outside of you.

I nodded politely but brushed it off along with the onslaught of well-meaning advice I received during pregnancy. It was such an odd thing, I thought, for someone to say. It was a notion I could not yet grasp. And then I had kids—four of them in eight years—and it turns out they were right.

～

I'm still here in the trenches of a charmed, messy life with littles, and I know our story is still evolving, unfolding like a well-wrapped gift. In another year, or seven, or even twelve, it will be a different story again: the rope of experience woven miles longer, my laugh lines deeper, my marriage tested and turned like a cord bearing different kinds of weight in different seasons.

This isn't a story about being done. It isn't a story about having it all figured out. It's a story about the pulse that runs through each of us: life constantly shifting, the ink barely drying on one chapter as the next unfolds, another storm brewing, the next season of rest awaiting.

When you gaze at yourself in the mirror, what exactly do you see? I see an imperfect yet capable, joy-filled mama, building and pursuing His Kingdom. And I see you just the same—as vulnerable as you are strong, as determined as you are flawed. All of us are His vessels, purposefully and intentionally equipped to raise little disciples as only we can.

We are, in every sense, jars of clay. We are fragile, yet we carry God's treasure. Here on earth, nothing parallels this more clearly than the experience of motherhood—witnessing our very own treasures growing within and outside of us—and one day, even leaving us.

I am overwhelmed at the thought of God's very hands crafting our lives. We often feel so weak, so at the mercy of the harshness of this world. Yet He trusts His most precious gifts to us—His message and His Spirit—and asks us to be the keepers of them.

We, too, must do the same with our children, knowing that as valuable and irreplaceable as they are, we have no choice but to send them out into a world that could so easily break them.

I don't know if you have had any close calls with your children. If you haven't yet, chances are, you will. Your children will likely crash and burn at some point, whether it's careening down a paved hill on their ten-speed bike, or flirting with rebellion in their teenage years, or staring down something truly heavy during adulthood. And they will likely find their faith being tested along the way. It's part of God's grand design, that just like every human on this earth, our children must choose to follow Him . . . or not.

You, as the person who knows their heart and loves them the deepest, will face a fork in the road, too. You will ask yourself the same questions I did: *How can it be that God trusts me with these babies—not only with their physical bodies, but most importantly, to make it my life's work to love them right back into His arms?* It is here that we must choose to surrender our children to their Creator. Otherwise, we will carry a burden through our mothering years that was never ours to carry.

~

Last spring, our eldest son had a couple of rough months at school. I watched him struggling, navigating friendships, authority, his own shortcomings, grappling under the weight of his own high expectations and pride. No matter what Scripture we spoke over him or how much we prayed, listened and corrected, I could see it wearing him down, his light growing a little dimmer each day.

After one particularly hard day, I crawled into bed next to my son after he fell asleep, put my hand on his warm chest, and rested my head on the pillow next to him. I stayed there beside him as long as I could, listening to the thump of his heart and the steady sound of his breathing, and my heart ached with the revelation that seemed so obvious until my child was hurting: *I'm not in control.*

How could I be this close to him, to all my kids—close enough to touch them every day, teach, admonish, encourage, kiss, defend, and discipline—yet feel so out of control when it came to their hearts? How must God feel the same, loving us so much, only to send us out into the world toddling around, racing, swerving from His loving arms. Does He hold His holy breath like every mother does?

This is what love does. It tethers you to a child you love as much as your own life, and takes you on a journey with them—to the heights to witness the blossoming of beautiful things, and to the depths where you have a front-row seat to the agony of their first disappointments and heartbreak. God knew, and still He designed motherhood exactly this way. *Doesn't that walk, that experience, draw us closer to Him?*

There is no place more vulnerable than parenting. You are stewarding not only your own heart, but someone else's. It is a tender, life-altering assignment, and I beg you to plant your feet, your heart and your soul in something so deep that the tilts and rough seas refine your muscles, that the hard days purify and clarify your mind and don't topple or dismantle what you have already built.

In that bathroom with Brooke's tiny, damp body pressed into my chest, my mind stunned at our brief brush with tragedy, I stood at a fork in the road in my walk with God. *What kind of mom did I really want to be? Did I trust myself? But deeper than that, did I trust Him?*

I didn't have all the answers that day, but I knew clearly that I didn't want to walk this road with fear, to spend decades of my life wrought with worry, anchored in anxiety. I had loved Jesus my whole life, but this felt different. I realized He had entrusted me with something of such great value—the privilege of stewarding the life of another human being—that it was too much to navigate on my own. This journey, He told me, would be clearer, sharper, more life-giving and free, if I did it *with Him*.

The shift that happened in my spirit was small, but it was significant enough to help me view the calling of motherhood with fresh eyes. I had a new urgency and desire not to miss what was right in front of me. I experienced the revelation that motherhood is all about the heart, and that it is possible, sweeter, fuller—even on the days that draw me to my knees—to parent with a spirit of *joy*.

CHAPTER TWO

AT THE WELL

Our friends own a ranch, and I tend to find excuses to be there; to stare out their back window and catch the hues of the sun awash on miles and miles of open pasture; to ride in the truck at springtime and discover a new calf, its wobbly legs and back slick with afterbirth; to climb up narrow, rickety stairs to the barn loft, close my eyes, and listen to the wind weave through the rafters.

I drop my eldest son off along with his muck boots, an extra pair of Levi's, and the sincere hope he will get on a horse by the end of the day. I linger in the kitchen where one of Jimmie's three tenacious daughters pulls an apple pie from the oven.

I stand in the entryway and breathe in the aroma of mud, wet dog hair, and the meatballs cooking for lunch, and I don't want to leave. My eldest son never wants to leave either. The open pastures, chickens pecking at the ground, rows of rhubarb plants, penned rabbits, what seem like open days of adventure, enthrall him. I remind him there are no days off here. Mornings come early. The work is relentless, sacrificial, difficult to measure, but deeply satisfying. I think my son loves the ranch for the same reason Jimmie loves her ranch. It touches people's souls, she tells me, because God is so very evident, so undeniable, in creation.

There's joy here, not happy-go-lucky smiles or simple good moods, but *real* joy born of discomfort and struggle, uncertainty and hardship.

And that's the secret about joy—it can exist amid sorrow and pain. Happiness cannot. We tend to confuse the two. Happiness is a flash-in-the-pan emotion—it's hot when it's hot. And when it's cold, it's gone. In his book, *Reliving the Passion*, author Walter Wangerin Jr. described it this way:

> "The difference between shallow happiness and a deep, sustaining joy is sorrow. Happiness lives where sorrow is not. When sorrow arrives, happiness dies. It can't stand pain. Joy, on the other hand, rises from sorrow and therefore can withstand all grief. Joy, by the grace of God, is the transfiguration of suffering into endurance, and of endurance into character, and of character into hope—and the hope that has become our joy does not (as happiness must for those who depend upon it) disappoint us."

God must want us to be happy, right? Absolutely. He's designed life to include happiness. And yet we usually end up chasing the fleeting high of happiness instead of long-lasting joy. I could give my kids a candy sucker every five minutes all day long to keep them happy, but I know what they really need is nutrition that will fuel their bodies and encourage long-term health. As children of God, we, too, need to stop chasing the 'suckers'—the people pleasing, the busyness, the material wealth—and, instead, seek the nourishment our souls truly crave. God knows that lasting happiness comes as we live according to His design.

I'm partly drawn to my friend's ranch just north of town because I miss my Wyoming childhood. There, in our tiny agricultural hub near the east gates of Yellowstone, meadowlarks perched on the fence. The ditches behind our house were lined with asparagus, and the fields were thick with alfalfa and beans. We hauled split logs from my dad's truck to an alcove next to the wood stove in our living room, tiny splinters lodging in our fingers. I have fond memories of my brother and I bottle-feeding a pet lamb, pushing each other around in a yellow paint-chipped wheelbarrow, and climbing into a straw hut to check on each new litter of kittens.

Yes, there's no doubt my friends' ranch reawakens memories of my Wyoming home. But something else resonates with me when I set foot onto their property.

It's the aroma of joy.

I like to think Jimmie has joy because of some inner strength molded by years of ranching—and this is partly true. However, I have also witnessed something more akin to a choice. She has learned to surrender her emotions to Jesus and give God the control which was never hers anyway—over the weather, over the cost of living, over all the ways the world tugs and pulls at what their family have worked for so many years to build.

I've seen the same surrender with other friends too—the one who said goodbye to her mother when cancer took her just months after the diagnosis, the one who held her newborn baby for a mere twenty minutes before handing his lifeless body over to a doctor, and the countless mothers around me who refuse to be rocked by the waves of their emotions, day in, day out, with each new high and low.

The aroma of joy permeates from each of these women because of their relationship with Jesus. They are not perfect, but they understand the need to anchor their hope in something bigger than themselves. These mothers who intentionally choose joy walk differently than the rest of the world. *Isn't that what our faith is supposed to look like? Shouldn't there be something different about those of us who love the Lord?*

These mothers find joy, not only in surrender, but in appreciating the little things in life. An incredible journey stretches out before us when we embark on motherhood, and it takes intentionality to do it well. After surrender, I cannot fathom any other way to experience each day with radical joy without this one thing: gratitude.

∼

Several years ago, I served in the infant and toddler room at church, and one Sunday we ended up with twice as many drop-offs as usual. It quickly turned into a marathon of diaper changes, wiping snotty noses, bottle-feeding, tears, and two diaper explosions (if you know, you know!).

I still remember that particular day because of the other volunteer in the room. Despite the chaos unfolding around us, this woman was radically joyful, overflowing with gratitude. It seemed to just bubble up from her. There's no other way to describe it. Almost every sentence out of her mouth was infused with an air of thankfulness. She spoke praise over every baby she held and found something positive to say to every parent she engaged with. In all the gross, thankless things we did that day, she focused on the good. She kept thanking Jesus for this baby's eyes, for that toddler's creative mind, for a building with air conditioning, for parents who care, for a church that gathers families. Her gratitude and praise changed the atmosphere of that room and brought a sense of calm to my spirit. I thought of her for days afterward.

She has since become a friend, and I've come to realize that it isn't that she is happy all the time. I've seen her mourn, express frustration, and face somber situations with the appropriate emotion. But beneath it all, there's a foundation of joy.

This year, speaking at a women's retreat, she shared her testimony about raising five children—one of them a prodigal. With boldness she described a turning point in her desire to lead him back to the Lord. She realized that her worship, her gratitude, her hallelujahs and her joy could not be stolen by *anything*. Period. If he didn't come back, she would still praise Jesus. If he made another mistake, she would still praise Jesus. Even if this hurt lasted forever, still she would praise Jesus.

Gratitude leads to joy. Every time.

This is evident in our parenting, too. Consistent thankfulness leads to the manifestation of joy. Every time I express gratitude for something, a muscle is being strengthened. These muscles are formed in the little things as much as they are in the big.

Outwardly, joy looks like many different things because it's truly a posture of the heart. It's an overflow of the Holy Spirit. It's also a choice. So is gratitude. Gratitude is a muscle to be flexed so consistently that it becomes our default mindset, an overflow of our heart's narrative. If something other than gratitude is in my heart, if my flesh is running the show, I know I need to return to the source of transformation. Christ is the well we must draw from, and the fruits of the Spirit—love, joy, peace, patience, kindness, goodness, faithfulness, gentleness and self-control—are the overflow of our intimate connection with Him. As a mom tasked with stewarding the hearts of my children as well as my own, and seeking to exude this aroma of joy in my everyday parenting, it is a connection I cannot live without.

～

I think of my mothering life as a blank canvas—stretched, clean, bare. Each moment of this lived-out calling is a stroke of color, a dot of detail. And when it's finished, when you're staring at this piece of art from a great distance, it may look as if the key features— the nose, the mouth, the eyes, for example—are what dominate the picture. You may think it's those big shifting moments, the tragedies, the celebrations, that make up the face of motherhood.

Then you step closer. Now you see that it's thousands upon thousands of delicate brush strokes, the everyday minutia of life, that actually compose much of the picture. You cannot be without either—those pivotal moments that changed the course of your life with your children, *or* the thousands of day-to-day brush strokes that slowly filled in and completed the canvas of your motherhood.

These brush strokes, the details you may have always considered to be the little things of life, matter. And if these small day-to-day moments are not also filled with joy, you risk leaving the pages of your picture blank—or worse, making destructive brush strokes that damage it altogether. It is when those defining moments of the picture enter your life and the storms strike, that you risk finding your joy-muscles weak and unprepared.

The emergency is hard. The crisis is hard. The tragedy is hard. *But do you know what's just as hard?* Drumming up the mental and emotional capacity to wake up each morning and pour out the fruits of the Spirit into the little people entrusted to you. Do you have it in you each day? Do you have the steely fortitude required to create an atmosphere of joy in your home—alongside the squabbles, the busyness, the ups and downs of emotions, the navigation of obedience and love?

I don't. Not on my own, anyway. And that, my friends, is why Jesus is the never-ending, always-available, always-overflowing well of joy. I'm standing at that well every day saying, "Lord, I need Your Spirit, Your grace. I need a sprinkle today, a cup, maybe even a gallon. In fact, can I just keep coming back to meet You here all day long?"

His answer is always *yes*.

Friend, can I be so bold as to ask: *What source are you drinking from?* Is it fear? Is it insecurity? Or is it contentment? Whatever it is that you comfortably slide to, that's your default setting. It was only when I learned to move the needle in my heart to a constant setting of joy that my world truly changed.

What are we risking? What is truly at stake? Does joy really matter in the midst of all we are called to do, and to do well? Please hear my heart. If there is truly a universal understanding among mothers, it is this: our most precious gift is time. Time is the greatest tool in our tool belt, yet it's also the great unknown.

Is there anything more sobering than the great expanse of time? We simply don't know how long we get with these kids God has given us. The clock is incessantly ticking. Just think, if . . . *if*, we get to parent our babies from their birth until they turn eighteen, we have 216 months, or 936 weeks, or 157,680 hours with them. *Just what exactly are we doing with this time?*

If we parent our kids without joy, we're wandering in circles. We are no different than the Israelites in the book of Exodus—grumbling, lost, hungry, aching—growing weary, pursuing but not finding purpose, knowing there was something better than this, but not quite able to claim it. This is not God's design or purpose for motherhood. It may be weighty and complicated, but it is not a burden. It's an honor, and it's one of the most poignant ways God draws us closer to Himself.

So how exactly do we access this well of joy? Well, we do it first by entering into a one-on-one relationship with Jesus, then by linking ourselves arm-in-arm with others. We do it by whittling away distractions. And we do it in spite of our fear.

~

Droughts are not novel events here in South Dakota. During the past decade, swathes of our region have experienced more than one severe drought—damaging crops, causing fires, stunting the growth of grass, and forcing ranchers and buffalo herd managers to sell off livestock.

Life was particularly arduous for ranchers last summer. Our land was in drought, extreme drought. The skies remained silent. The ponds dried up. The land became scorched and cracked, and the damage was done. My friend's husband endured months of exhaustion locating and securing sources of water, then hauling truckload after truckload to their animals. It's painstaking work.

I couldn't help but think of him as I traveled to Missouri earlier this year. Missouri is the home of the natural 'Big Spring'. The largest spring in the world, it forcefully churns out millions of gallons of crystal-clear water each year, growing ever larger as it erodes the limestone walls surrounding it. What my ranching friends wouldn't have given for even a small piece of that spring, for the chance to offer their cows access to clean, flowing water every minute of every day, for the rest of their lives.

Then, just last month, contractors traveled out to my friend's ranch on a mission to fix the archaic pump that had been installed years earlier to draw water from one of the deep underground wells on their property. I know my friend had lost sleep over this well, because if it wasn't repaired, they faced yet another summer of hauling water, yet another summer of parched, thirsty cattle roaming their land. Yet another summer of heartache.

My friend called me later that day, overwhelmed with gratitude. On her phone she had captured a picture of the contractors and her daughters all crowded around a hole in the ground from which the most beautiful fount of water was sprouting up, soaking the parched land beneath their feet.

That is exactly what Jesus offers us. Mothers cannot manifest a lifelong source of stamina, patience and joy unless we tap into the ancient spring—Christ Himself! We weren't designed to do this on our own, in our own strength. *Where do we get the idea that this is desirable, or even possible?* We need Jesus. Period.

∼

Jesus masterfully used water as an analogy when He conversed with the woman at the well, an account we read about in the gospel of John. In Jesus' time, women traveled to the local well daily to draw water and share life together. This Samaritan woman picked a time of day when not many other women would have been there. *Why?* Perhaps she liked her time alone. Or maybe there was a deeper reason—like not wanting to face uncomfortable questions about her lifestyle and the fact she was living with a man who was not her husband.

On this particular day when she went to the well, Jesus and His disciples were heading north from Jerusalem to Galilee. Hot, hungry and thirsty, the disciples kept going another half a mile to the village of Sychar to find food, but Jesus stopped at the well. There, He met the Samaritan woman. Interestingly, Jesus did not condemn her or mention her sin. Instead, He reminded her that there was more for her than what she could taste, see and feel—a source of life that never runs dry. During their short conversation, Jesus said something that very likely changed the trajectory of her entire life—He invited her to drink of 'living water', water that would spring up and satisfy her so she might never thirst again.

~

With Jesus as our source of living water, there are never dry times. He never holds back. Sometimes the joy comes easily, bubbling up and over like that Big Spring in Missouri. Other times you have to dig deep; you have to go out of your way to cultivate a life of joy. On those days, you must lean in and do the hard work. Sometimes, you, mama, have to haul the water!

I have done life with moms who walk around in a state of despair, a haze. The day-to-day struggles of life have left a foggy film over their eyes. They cannot see the beauty anymore. They cannot muster the strength or energy to find something positive to say. They are drained and cornered. My heart hurts for them.

Hear me when I say I'm not talking about just having a bad day or navigating a painful season. There are going to be some barely-holding-on seasons, and that's okay. I'm not talking about clinically diagnosed mental health issues either. Friends, if you are dealing with depression or another mental health condition, this is an entirely separate issue than a lack of joy. Please get professional help if you need it.

What I'm talking about is loving the Lord, having a life-giving relationship with Jesus Christ, and waking up every morning ready to surrender negative thought patterns or attitudes and take a stand against the spirit of fear. This is how we engage in seeking joy. It involves a soul-shift, a dropping off of the scales from your eyes, a complete surrender to God who wants you to be joy-filled as you walk through life. As mothers, this is one of the most important actions we can take. It's how we lead by example, it's how we set the atmosphere of our home, it's how we navigate stressful moments without making things worse. We learn to draw from the source!

So, I'm asking you mama, *where is your joy?* What is your aroma? What do people sense when they are around you?

God set you apart. He set this day apart. Psalm 118:24 says, "This is the day the Lord has made: let us rejoice and be glad in it." He created this day, so let's not waste it. Let's not choose to live our life, mother our kids, and steward our family and home, in a self-induced drought. *How many times have we walked past the well of joy? If Christ is truly our unending source of stability in the chaos, why don't we drink?*

There is an end to what we can do. There is a limit. Some days we feel that we simply cannot go on any longer, or that we cannot do this job well anymore.

And even then, He is beside us, offering His never-ending, life-giving joy. So please keep going, friend. We have everything we need to mother with joy right at our fingertips. But first we must come to the well, and drink.

CHAPTER THREE

TOWERS

"Go. Spread out. Explore. Build homes. Have babies. Enjoy."

This was God's desire for His people following the devastating flood in the book of Genesis. It was a directive to move, plant seeds, and build families.

Their response: "Let's stay right here and build a tower to Heaven."

And that's what they did. They plopped down their suitcases, set up shop, and got to work.

The history of the Tower of Babel fascinates me because this first group of people who had free rein on the earth to chart new territories, move about freely, scale mountains, cross deserts and start afresh, decided to settle instead.

And they said, "Come, let us build ourselves a city, and a tower whose top is in the heavens; let us make a name for ourselves, lest we be scattered abroad over the face of the whole earth."
Genesis 11:4 NKJV

They were playing a dangerous game. Motivated by pride, they began designing, building and controlling their way to their own destiny. They figured they could do it better their way. They felt they needed to do something permanent and impressive and claim it as their own feat, or else they would be scattered, weakened, and vulnerable. Simply put, they wanted to carve out their own identity. They craved control.

Sound familiar, mamas? This desire for control can become especially acute when we have our own babies to care for and protect. I wonder if we, as Christian mothers, even when we are seemingly on the right track, ever allow an identity or passion, a job, a schedule or a conviction to become a tower? What towers might we have wearily and painstakingly built by hand, determined to make progress in an area that God never anointed or maybe never desired for us to build right now? When did we inadvertently settle, set up shop, and start building towers to Heaven?

~

As a child, I remember nights in bed, the darkness enveloping my room slowly as my mind picked over my two greatest fears—my parents dying, or my parents divorcing. It seemed that if one of those two things happened, my entire world would unravel like a ball of yarn coming undone with one snip of the scissors.

At night, my door stayed cracked open an inch, just enough to see my parents curled up on the couch together watching TV. If I couldn't see them, I would tiptoe to the door, my feet sinking into pale pink carpet, and wait. Tethered to their presence, my rest was suspended until they were back in their usual spots.

My parents taught me about Jesus, but in reality I worshipped at the altar of pleasing *them*. I desperately wanted to be good. Disappointing them felt awful. My parents were my source of stability, a haven of warmth, and I absorbed their direction and guidance with great care.

And so it came as an incredible shock to me when, on a windless, blue-skied day in the middle of October, my father packed boxes into his red Chevrolet and my mother sat tear-stained and trembling at the top of the stairs. In that moment, the world shifted beneath my feet.

I was sixteen, a sophomore in high school, when the nightmare I had harbored as that night-gowned little girl whose childhood was firmly anchored in Mom and Dad, unfolded before me. My father was leaving, and a divorce would soon follow.

I believed in Jesus, but up until that point I had clung to my parents' faith—*they* were my tower. Every day, I jumped in the water with a flotation device—my parents were my buoy, a consistent marker in the waves.

An hour earlier, sitting on the bed next to my father as he told me the news, I had been flung into the deep. It was my first tragedy. I heard his words, and they rolled around in my head, but my mind couldn't settle on them. They were like hot coals I desperately wanted to hand back to him. They seemed so out of place in our home, in that room.

I stared at his blue eyes. The air was suddenly electric and hot, my stomach was clenched in a fist, my throat dry. I couldn't take

27

a breath—it was as if all the oxygen had been sucked out of the room. *Jesus, I can't even breathe. You're going to have to inhale and exhale for me.*

That day, a core piece of my identity was uprooted in my heart. My heart ached in a way I didn't know was possible. Something had just been taken from me, and I couldn't get it back. Like a balloon slipping from my fingers, it was already floating away. Something had been set in motion that couldn't be reversed.

A friend later told me I needed to grieve their separation and divorce like it was a death, and I realized they were right. It was the death of our family. The death of an identity. The death of what I thought the future looked like for all of us. It was a tower coming undone. In that tender season I learned one of life's most terrifying—and wonderful—truths: people, even your favorite people, will fail you at some point. God never will.

As with all tragedies, the world does not, in fact, fall apart when something bad happens. Now, as I look back on my parents' marriage and divorce two decades later, I am grateful they loved Jesus and taught me to love Him too. When they divorced, as deeply as it wounded me, I clung to the One they had taught me to lean on—the One who would never let me down.

～

When my husband and I bought our first house, my dad came to visit. As we stood out in the front yard with the smell of fresh grass clippings and the nearby cattle lingering as the sun dipped behind the tree line, a swell of grief suddenly washed over me. I started to cry, and I couldn't stop. I wiped away tears and smudged the wet on my jeans. I thought about another time when I stood before him, hurting, not sure how to articulate what I felt.

One weekend, years earlier, my parents took us to the local Pizza Hut for dinner. My brother and I sat across from each other in the booth, kicking each other's shins, flicking the red flecks of hot pepper out of the shakers, and burning our tongues on the simmering top layer of cheese. I remember the restaurant was promoting a movie called *Fern Gully* that day, and I proudly left with a tiny tree tucked underneath my arm. Dad and I planted it that summer, and watched it take root in our backyard.

One night as we were tossing the baseball back and forth near the fledgling tree, the ball bounced off the tip of my glove and popped me in the mouth. My lip swelled and I was choking back tears, yet I paced in front of my dad, waving off his concern and pretending it didn't hurt. What I remember most about that backyard ball game was not my busted lip, however—it was how desperately I wanted to not hurt my dad's feelings. It was one of the first times I realized the tenderness of my heart for my parents. I couldn't bear the thought of disappointing them or causing them any sort of grief.

Now I was a grown adult standing in front of my first house, yet still I didn't want to hurt my dad. I drew circles in the dirt of the driveway with my toe, willing my emotions under control as I realized that all the milestones I had envisioned with my parents standing together beside me—at my high school graduation, tacking posters to the cement wall in my college dorm, dancing on my wedding day, proudly showing off my first house—were coming and going.

When we'd bought this house, a three-bedroom ranch on the outskirts of Rapid City, South Dakota, my mom came to organize my cabinets, lay out the rugs, and help unpack the boxes. My dad came a couple of months later. He walked around with me, checking out the yard, looking at the siding. But they should have been there together, and the loss of those moments grieved me deeply.

So, I stood in the driveway with my dad that day and told him exactly that. Then I forgave him, again. That day, as I received his heartfelt apology for causing me pain, the heaviness in my chest lightened.

$\sim$

The pain of the towers we have built in our lives coming down is never wasted. It's where God heals and rebuilds like a master potter, molding the ashes of our hurt into something redeemed.

Fifteen years into my own marriage, I am struck by God's power to heal and restore. I love to sit with my dad for hours, staring at those same slate-blue eyes as we discuss and debate our views on free will, and the role of politicians in today's society, and whether churches should have coffee shops. I bring him pistachios and banana cream pie for his birthdays, and we talk about old family vacations and the economy and raising kids. I just entered my forties and I feel this time shrinking; the tension of change is on the horizon, and I am desperate for more.

It is like rock striking rock when I get into theology discussions with my dad, and I come out more refined, more polished, more on fire, even when we don't agree. He is the ultimate skeptic—a fact, he says, that has cemented his faith. There were no commentaries, no statistics, no history lessons that convinced my dad that Jesus is real, only an encounter with God Himself.

And my mom—who rose from the staircase that day my dad left, took me by the hand, and helped me out of the deep—is a companion of hope. She is a pulsating heart: the encourager, the listener, the soft place I land. She is my best friend, a voice in my head and on the phone, and always hugging me. Always, always hugging me.

She loves people well and hard. During my childhood she was a master of encouragement, placing handwritten notes in my lunch box, present at every performance, the first to tell me I should put pen to paper and write. Now she is the person I call when I can't remember the rhubarb cake recipe, when one of the kids is having an allergic reaction, when I've just said yes to a new editor. She is so deeply a part of me, and I see this full circle now—what she felt as a mother, I now feel as a mother. I fear that losing her someday will leave an irreplaceable gap in my life, like losing one of my hands, leaving me to function with only part of myself.

~

The older I get, the more I sense that little girl in me wanting to build yet another tower, this time for *my* own family, for *my* own kids. There's a magnetic pull moms feel to want to be everything to their kids: to create every promise of stability, to pluck and pull and build a safe nest for them. A nest that says, *I will never leave you. Nothing bad will ever happen. You are safe with me.*

But those desires are not always realistic. These beautiful babies aren't really ours; they are His. He designed the people we love to be woven into the permanent fabric of our lives, not to serve as the rock to build our lives upon. Jesus is the only solid rock. If there was ever a moment in my life that shook me to my core enough to see that truth clearly, it was the breakup of my family. My tower.

Have you hit your fork in the road yet? Not just about a big decision—the job, or the marriage, or the house—but the one where you question if He is real, if He actually is who He says He is. I asked that question while sitting on my bed at sixteen: *If you're here God, I need you to show up now. If not, I'm out.* He showed up that day, and every day since.

If you haven't reached that point yet, you will. He will always pursue our hearts. He is a Father in pursuit of His children.

If you are building towers to secure an identity, or because you're distracted, or because you think you can build a fortress that is safer than where God has called you, know that His way is always better. Every high thing in our lives that is not of Him will eventually come down. Maybe it is people pleasing. Maybe you have made your family a tower. Or your finances, or ministry, or business. Maybe you have decided, with an unknowing arrogance, that you can do this on your own. You can't, friend, you can't. And if you don't humble yourself, He will. Isaiah 2:12-18 says,

The Lord Almighty has a day in store for all the proud and lofty, for all that is exalted (and they will be humbled), for all the cedars of Lebanon, tall and lofty, and all the oaks of Bashan, for all the towering mountains and all the high hills, for every lofty tower and every fortified wall, for every trading ship and every stately vessel. The arrogance of man will be brought low and human pride humbled; the Lord alone will be exalted in that day, but the idols will disappear. (NIV)

Perhaps the tower that needs to come down is something He ordained in the beginning. Maybe it's a ministry, a move, a job, a project, or a mentorship relationship, and now He is dismantling it. That season—the one you took the step toward in obedience and partnered with God to create—is now over. It's time to move on.

I don't know about you, but I don't want to settle. I don't want man-made towers. I want a fire in my bones to move, to hear the Holy Spirit, and to boldly guide our kids to go where God tells them to go. Building towers is much like chasing contentment, looking for happiness in man-made designs. When our 'tower' is God Himself, there we will experience the true source of joy.

CHAPTER FOUR

THE BETTER PORTION

The inside of a tornado is called 'the death zone', and not because of the flying debris, lightning bolts, and walls of wind. It's given this name because the very center of a tornado is freezing cold and has little oxygen.

In short, you can't breathe, and you suffocate.

I spent time in that space early in my motherhood journey when there appeared to be a collision of one part of my life with another. I stumbled along, trying to acclimate, longing to do motherhood well, but unwilling to let go of the work and passions I had spent years cultivating. I wanted to work full-time at a job I deeply loved, squeeze in hobbies, lead and serve, and still be a rock star mom. I wanted it all.

From childhood, I longed to be a mother. And now here I was, babies in my arms, wholly sure it was right and that the puzzle pieces of my life were finally snapping into place. *So why was the best thing that had ever happened to me causing such confusion in my heart?* I searched for answers in the wrong places, getting advice from well-meaning people who thought I was pursuing productivity. I wasn't.

I needed rest. I needed space. I needed to learn to say no.

When I became a mom, I was certain I could continue at the pace I had lived before and simply add kids like an addendum to my life, cramming as much as possible into every nook and cranny. But if you are a mother, you know the truth—with children, the rhythm of life drastically shifts.

We talk often about the incredible moment of the birth of a baby, but we should also talk about the birth of a mother with equal weight, for in the miraculous, painful, luminous moment that your baby enters the world, the fibers of your own being stretch, reshape, and transform. You're never quite the same.

I know I'm not alone in my thinking. I look around and I see other mothers trapped in the middle of a swirling life, not fully planted anywhere. They are convinced they can do it all, but in reality, they are suffocating. There's no fullness of joy, because God has called us to something new, and we haven't yet embraced it.

Inside my own tornado, I pep-talked my way into a lot of tower-building: *I deserve this career. I can have time for my husband and maintain the side hustle, and support my friends, and host the Bible study, and travel with the dance team, and cook and clean, and work out and eat healthy, and say yes and yes and yes.*

I was lying to myself.

I resisted the idea that reorienting my life for motherhood was healthy, right, and might even be the very ministry He was calling me to. I listened with bated breath to the well-meaning advice of believers and unbelievers alike who let it be known, through a side comment or a raised brow, that they thought it second-best to put a career on hold to stay home, or to adjust your schedule around your kids.

I don't want to lie anymore, and I don't want to lie to you. *We can't have it all.* There, I said it. Read it again. We can't have it all—at least, not everything, all at once, in every season, as society would have us believe. Besides, who said that was the best thing for us anyway?

I want us to 'have it all' in the sense that I want us to experience all that God has promised—what He *really* promised—not what the world would have us believe is owed to us. He offers us a faithful relationship with Him, soaked in His goodness and overflowing with joy. It's something I needed before kids, and I desperately need it now that I'm a mom.

∼

Motherhood is beautiful. It's colorful. It's hard.

When I became a mother, it was as if someone took all the separate paint cans of my life and poured all the paint into one cardboard box. The clean, the controlled, the 'everything-fits' life quickly evaporated, and instead I was pouring out all over the seams, soaking into the cardboard, and staining everything around me.

I talked with a friend recently about how our identities shifted with the onset of motherhood. She's a TV personality: quick-witted, talented, attractive, magnetic. And when she had babies, she faced the same internal struggle: *I look in the mirror and I see the same person, but I'm not her anymore. Or am I?*

One of my best friends from high school is now a mother of five. When her youngest started school, she sat in her living room that first week, a bit stunned by this sudden shift of quiet time—a little space to breath, the ache of them not there—and she didn't even know what to do with herself. *I'm not sure who I am without my kids.*

There are core questions that impress on the minds and hearts of so many moms I know: *Do I stay home or go back to work? Do I say yes or no to all the presses and pulls of my time, my energy, and my resources? Mercy, how do I balance it all in a delicate equilibrium?*

How easy it is to get stuck in a bubble, spinning and running and working and being mommy. We become too dizzy to look up at Him and be obedient. We become too distracted, fearful, and busy to plant our roots down deep into the fertile soil of strong, authentic relationships.

When we shower our pregnant mamas, why don't we, along with the cake and the onesies, shower them with confirmation and encouragement that when they hold that baby for the first time, a new work has begun? God has fashioned something new and unfamiliar, designed just the way He planned, and they'll soon feel it bubbling up and over in their spirit and their soul.

Mamas, you are not lost. You are not losing your way. You are not alone. Look at this verse from the book of Isaiah: "When you pass through the waters, I will be with you; and through the rivers, they shall not overwhelm you; when you walk through fire you shall not be burned, and the flame shall not consume you. For I am the Lord your God, the Holy One of Israel, your Savior" (Isaiah 43:2).

Later in the chapter, God reminds us that all things are under His authority. Motherhood is under His authority. He's building a new thing. And when the path stretches out in front of us, He will make a way: "Behold I am doing a new thing, now it springs forth; do you not perceive it? I will even make a way in the wilderness, and rivers in the desert" (Isaiah 43:19).

It has taken years, four babies, and a lot of letting go to step out of my tornado, to breathe, and to finally get a grip on this. We are women who have been called to motherhood, so let's not live in the middle, but be 'all in'. Let's be open to who He wants us to become.

∼

I started dance early. In my kindergarten ballet class, I pouted and fidgeted with my tutu onstage. Apparently the dances weren't fast-paced or the music loud enough for me.

But at the age of eight, I slipped on my first pair of clogging shoes, and when the metal taps struck the floor and the percussive rhythm synced with the beats of the music, I was a light bulb plugged in—electric and alive.

I learned the first couple of steps with ease, and soon I was dancing in the house, at the grocery store; my feet running sequences beneath my desk at school, my legs a-flutter during dinner. I progressed through the classes quickly, challenged by the rhythm and the choreography, driven by the excitement of performance.

My parents and my brother took classes too, and my parents moved their stereo to the garage to practice. I would listen to the metal *ting* of their shoes hitting the concrete, the studied look of concentration set on their faces.

During the summer, my whole family, along with our dance group, drove past Cody, up into the North Fork to a ranch to perform for tourists making their way to Yellowstone. The only hard surface for our taps was the outdoor tennis court, and visitors unfolded lawn chairs, clapped along to the music, and asked about our shoes.

I ended performances sweaty and trembling, my body abuzz with adrenaline. I felt free onstage. I had mastered the songs for a purpose—to bring something good and interesting and inspiring. It felt natural, like running. The songs unfurled in front of me, rolling out like the tide, and when I finished the last step, when the wave had crashed over me, there was a sweet release. I could go home and sleep deep and well.

On the way back from the ranch we would stop at Dairy Queen for ice cream. Year after year, practice after practice, trip after trip, our fellow dancers loved on our family and became our friends. They cheered me on in high school and attended my graduation, my wedding.

In my senior year of high school, my instructor moved away and handed me the reins of the business. I felt honored, responsible. The idea that I could be paid for doing something I loved, using the gift God had given me, was a revelation.

Clogging has been woven into my life story for three decades now. I pursued a writing career and earned a journalism degree, but never stopped dancing. I have clogged all over the United States, Spain, the Caribbean. I moved to Montana for college and taught clogging at the university where I studied. Each time I moved, I started a new studio, traveled to workshops, and kept performing.

And so, when I had babies, I kept dancing. I kept writing and serving at church and, as always, trying to do too much. I ignored a nagging feeling, a God whisper: *It's time. It's time to release some of this.*

Six weeks after an emergency C-section with our first baby, I took to the stage at a performance, my body still aching, my incision still tender.

As our family grew, I took each baby along as I taught multiple classes a week. I breastfed between classes, pumped milk in the dusty, cramped storage closet, strapped them to my chest in a pouch until they dozed off. My dancers hosted a baby shower and doted on our kids, and it was their friendship, my loyalty to a growing business, and an unfailing pride that caused me to keep going.

"How," I asked God, "could You ask me to give up something I love? Something that is so good?" And this, my friends, is how my tower was built. My pride led my will: *I can do this at the pace*

I was doing it before—even with kids. Look at me, I can do it all. Pride sure is an ugly, deceitful thing.

When my third baby was six months old, I took my dance team to perform in Disneyland. On top of managing our dancers and their families, I lugged a car seat, stroller and diaper bag, and paced in the hotel room for hours every night to get him to sleep. I skipped the rides and rocked him to sleep in the heat, breastmilk and sweat soaking into my bra pads. Happy but exhausted, I felt torn.

∼

I've heard it said that mommy-guilt is real and no matter what you do, you will always feel it. You must, therefore, choose the activity that gives you less of it. I can relate to this mindset because I've felt it too—that throb in your heart when you travel and leave them at home, when your toddler crawls into your lap but you just can't break from your work right at that moment.

But let me say this: Just because you're apart from your kids and miss them doesn't mean it's necessarily mom-guilt. The word 'guilt' implies you've done something wrong.

We are called to simply be obedient to Christ, whether that means working outside the home or quitting your job, staying home or traveling, finishing your work before you pick up your child, or sensing they need a hug right then. If we stay true to what He has called us to in each season and genuinely operate in partnership with the Holy Spirit, we don't have to walk in guilt or inadequacy, or any other feelings of condemnation we like to strap on and carry around as women.

Are you doing what God called you to do this season, regardless of your paycheck, what your friends are doing, what was preached at church, what your parents say, what kind of childhood experience you had? If you are obedient first and last and always, He's going to cover every gap.

I've thought a lot about the concept of mom-guilt these last couple of years, and it has led me to saying sorry, a lot. I don't think sorry is said enough in our world. It's a diffuser of tense situations, a salve for the wound, a re-direction for a minor infraction, momentum in the right direction when you have caused deep pain.

It can also mean nothing when you've said it too much. And I've said it too much. I look back on the first years as a mother and I wince when I think of how many times I mumbled the word, "sorry." *Sorry I'm late. Sorry he spit up on you. Sorry I missed the story deadline. Sorry my hair and make-up aren't done. Sorry I forgot. Sorry I'm low on energy. Sorry. Sorry. Sorry.*

It was one of the reasons I quit my job. I realized I was going to spend a whole lot of time saying sorry to both sides—the people at home, and the people at work. I didn't want to say sorry anymore. So, I either had to change the things that led to the sorry, or stop saying sorry. If I don't really want to change, the sorry isn't genuine anyway. I don't need to offer shallow apologies, and I certainly don't need to feel guilty if I'm walking in obedience.

I don't regret that trip to Disneyland. I don't regret any of my time with my dancers, but I do regret my disobedience to Jesus during that time. Back then, I couldn't see a clear way to keep the studio going without closing it, so I muscled on. I ignored God's voice.

Even as I kept building my tower, I kept talking to God. And He kept listening. With precise patience, He pressed on my heart over and over that it was time to let go. It was at a New Year's Eve party a few years later when it finally dawned on me: the longer I was disobedient, the more I was pulling back from His protection and His blessing.

~

It's become tradition in our home to spend the final night of the year with our furniture pushed to the walls in the living room, the sun going down on friends and charades, sparkling cider, and white chicken chili. Our home is full and warm and relaxed on New Year's Eve, like we're standing on the cusp of something fresh, hand-in-hand with our favorite people, expectant, hopeful, released.

And so it was, in late 2019—with the temperatures dropping rapidly and a thin layer of snow collecting on the windshields of the cars, the kids weaving in and out of our legs, racing down and back up the stairs—that the men moved to a far corner of the room, and the conversation with my girlfriends turned to Jesus.

The trendy thing was to pick a word for the coming year, something buzzy like "purpose" or "rise". I had asked God to reveal a word—something encouraging and powerful, moving and catchy. But He didn't give me a word. He gave me the book of Luke.

As I read and reread Luke's gospel, I found my wheels spinning on the passage about Mary and Martha. It's a simple story: Jesus was a houseguest in Martha's home, and she scurried about getting dinner prepared, the kitchen cleaned, the bread baked. But for her sister Mary, there was no hustle, no hurry. Instead, she sat at Jesus' feet.

Martha chose the work. Mary chose the treasure. She chose the good, the better portion.

It seemed as if those words leapt off the page as soon as I read them, yet still I tried negotiating with God. *Things are good right now. We're on cruise control. I'm tired God, yes, but I can be this busy, because, really, everything in my schedule, every portion is good.*

I was wrong. As mothers, we are called to the good portion, not *every* portion. He doesn't call us to live on autopilot, where it's easy for our faith to grow lukewarm and our relationships to stall. There's no joy in operating on autopilot.

Sometimes we clutch the good so tightly we miss grabbing hold of the great, and that's precisely what I was doing. Like that picture a friend once gave me of a little girl holding onto a small teddy bear and Jesus kneeling in front of her with a larger teddy bear behind His back, His hand was outstretched as if to say, "Please let go of what you are so desperately holding on to so I can give you something greater."

I told my friends that December night, with a new revelation fluttering in my chest, that God had told me to "choose the good portion." I had always felt like motherhood, just by itself, wasn't enough, and maybe deep down I thought that when I looked at other women, too. *You're a great mom, but what are you 'doing'?* Speaking this out loud, to this group of friends, where I knew

I could be vulnerable and honest, imprinted something in my heart. It was time to let go of my schedule—*more work, more money, more toys, more food, more ministry*—and give Him the space to give me the better portion, the things that fill my soul and bring long-lasting joy. The things that create in me a new heart and ultimately build His Kingdom.

CHAPTER FIVE

HOT MESS

The good intentions I had proclaimed over the coming year were instantly put to the test. God must have known I wouldn't step back willingly, that I would fight for every tower—justify every busy day, resist the stripping down of our schedule, the reprioritizing, the fresh look at our life—because He took it out of my hands. A couple of months later, in early 2020, the Covid-19 pandemic hit.

Around the country, things rapidly shut down. My small businesses stuttered to a stop. Our school closed. Our church moved online. My entire calendar cleared. It was a stunning reversal to the otherwise busy and chaotic life we led. It was a pivot. It felt like a miracle.

We had less money coming in, but I felt wealthier. Our evenings and weekends had been jam-packed with school activities, sports, dance classes and service projects. Now it was all on hold. We were simply home. Yet, I didn't feel stuck at home; I felt rested. I built more blanket forts, Lego towers, and marshmallow stick people. I cooked more meals—zucchini lasagna, stuffed chicken ricotta, my grandma's zucchini cake and banana bread. Elijah discovered a knack for making homemade popcorn on the stove. Jonah kept me at his bedside longer at bedtime. I chased the kids in the back yard more often, rode bikes to the pond, stirred purple slime, folded paper airplanes, read more books. I listened closer, left space for silence, and spoke carefully and openly when they asked questions about a cuss word they heard at the park or wondered about their body.

I'm not delusional; this was no fairytale. There was also more fighting, more messes, more stepping on each other's toes. But when there's space and time, you have the capacity, the extra *oomph* to deal with the things that rub us against one other and build a strong foundation on which your family can grow.

I was forced into a time of rest. I was forced into a time of renewal. I realized, perhaps for the first time, that I was not drained because of my kids; I was drained because of all the running around.

Shortly after we returned to in-person church services, our pastor delivered his sermon with a small dinner table behind him, all set up with candles and chairs and linens. He wanted to illustrate the reality of Psalm 23, "You prepare a table before me in the presence of my enemies; you anoint my head with oil; my cup overflows" (v. 5). I knew God was inviting me to return to His table, not in a rush, with fast food and cheap pretenses, but slowly and quietly to sit awhile with Him. Why? Because He's God. Because He took the time to prepare. Because He loves me and knows I need space and rest, and I need to model that lifestyle for my kids, too.

The positive changes our family experienced in no way diminish the fact that the pandemic wreaked havoc on innumerable lives and ushered in a season of grief for many people. I honor those situations. But the Covid pandemic also brought clarity. And when the dust settled for our family, that clarity meant not returning to the schedule we had lived before.

I felt lighter than I had in years. So, in a first bold step toward obedience, I asked my dear friend Joelene to pray about taking over my clogging business. This capable, energetic sister in Christ had danced alongside me for a decade and a half, and she supported me when I said I needed a change. The studio is now hers.

It's still so fresh. A woman recognized me in the grocery store last week and asked if I was "the clogging lady". My heart caught in my throat for a second before I could respond. It's a bittersweet acknowledgment—I still teach, but that business is no longer mine. I get to dance with my friends and travel when it works with our family's schedule, but I am not in charge. There's a lightness, a freedom in that. It turns out God knew what He was doing all along.

～

We all need rest. But we don't rest, do we? We don't do boundaries well. We don't say no well. We don't ask for help well. We simply don't know how to stop.

God designed us to be purposeful in rest, to intentionally build margin and space into our lives. Yet somehow we have ignored the greatest cue God could have given us: *Here's your seven days, please rest on one, just one.*

Busyness is like the crack cocaine of motherhood. The adrenaline, the pride, the false sense of security it brings—that's the high. And it's right where Satan wants us, sucked up into every swirling tornado around us, never truly grounded.

The term "rat race" was coined in the 1930s to describe the futile, endless race between rats who scurried from room to room, trying to outpace each other to get to the piece of cheese. Trainee fighter pilots also used the term to describe the process of following the leader, copying all the actions, loops, snap rolls and tighter turns of an experienced pilot.

We are just like that sometimes. We spend all our energy trying to keep up, and we use it as an excuse to not stop and deal with our emotions, cultivate healthy habits, or get our priorities in order. Our families suffer because of it. *We* suffer because of it.

What are you chasing? If you have filled your schedule so tight that you do not have time to be in God's Word, or pray, or enjoy your relationships, it means you are not pursing the good portion. It's too tight. Period.

I have stopped saying, "Oh, we're so busy," because it's something I have desperately sought to change in our home. Our lives are full, but I want them to be full of the *right* things.

If I'm being honest, I need to continue to ask myself if I care more about raising disciples of Jesus or about trying to have good, well-behaved kids—kids who can do things and be things and accomplish things—because it makes me look like a good mother.

When I need to refocus, I train my eyes and my heart on the fact that I deeply desire for my kids to know Jesus and to never live a single day without pursuing that relationship. And when I find myself worried about what others think; when I'm worried my kids aren't involved in enough activities; when my eyes are fixed on the lives of other moms instead of my own, I get on my knees, repent, and reset my heart on the goal of raising disciples.

The football practice, the tennis lessons, the cheerleading, the basket weaving classes may benefit your kids emotionally and physically, teach them teamwork, and help them persevere. But do you know what will really help your kiddos? A mom who is in the Word, who chooses wisely, knows when to say no, has the capacity to disciple because she is not distracted, chooses the good portion, and experiences joy. That is a worthy legacy to pursue, mamas. They might not play basketball forever, but your kids will need Jesus, forever.

My generation has confused busyness and stress with an excellent life. It's trendy these days to pack your schedule so tight that you show up everywhere in a crazed heap. It's cool, desirable even, to be the mom who is a hot mess. I get it, it's kind of humorous. I may even have the mug to match. But it's also sad. All mothers have hot-mess days, but God has designed us to be so much more than that.

Do you ever feel caught in that cycle of never being satisfied? We want more and more and more. It's why I fill my schedule. If it is full, it must be good. If I'm hustling to earn it, it must be worthy of my exhaustion.

In his book, *A Hunger for God,* John Piper wrote, "The greatest enemy of hunger for God is not poison but apple pie. It is not the banquet of the wicked that dulls our appetite for Heaven, but endless nibbling at the table of the world."

In some ways, being a busy mom is a badge of honor. Some of us may even be addicted to the stress. It is possible to become addicted to your own hormones—the adrenaline and cortisol that pumps through your body when you operate in stress. When this is the case, entering a season of rest actually causes unease.

Stress works in much the same way as a drug—not only is it addictive, it causes our hearts to race, our blood pressure to rise. We can end up with digestive problems, ulcers, panic attacks . . . the list is endless.

And no wonder we are stressed. The average American home has tripled in size over the course of our lifetime, and we fill them with clutter. In fact, one in ten Americans now rent offsite storage!

Moms, we want the best for our kids, but do not be deceived. We serve a God of order and intention, not gluttony and slop. We have an insatiable appetite for bigger, for better, for more. We stuff our schedules, we stuff our bellies, yet still we starve. Our faith stagnates, our marriages strain under the pressure, and our joy is depleted.

I want my kids to engage in a real one-on-one relationship with Jesus Christ above all else—the schooling, the art lessons, the football games, the friendships, the career dreams, the fishing trips, the research papers, the swimming lessons . . . I want all of it to be relegated to its proper place—and that certainly shouldn't be number one. For if we overpack their schedules but they have no eternal hope, what are we doing?

There will always be days when the kids throw up, the dishwasher breaks, we forget the dentist appointment, and things unravel fast. But there's a difference between having a day here and there when we just can't seem to get it together and creating a life that is so overflowing with commitments and material possessions that we become habitually stressed out and exhausted. We've become moms who have forsaken our joy.

~

Perfume was the final straw for me. Chanel N°5 to be exact.

It was simple. I was in love with our new baby yet also enamored with my job as a journalist. As soon as my maternity leave was over, I packed up my notebooks and breast pump and headed back to my desk at the newsroom.

When I look back now, *who was I kidding?* We all know it's not that simple. It's complicated—or perhaps we make it so—when we have babies yet want to return to work. I went back to my job that day, but not without deep conflict in my heart.

Some things came together easily. My friend's mother-in-law offered to babysit Elijah the first year he was born. She lived on a property out in the country with her girls. It was a great environment for Elijah, and I was thrilled. It seemed all the pieces were falling into place. Every piece except my peace. I just didn't have it.

The first few months after I returned to work, I spent my evenings on the couch, my stomach still soft from pregnancy, my eyes burning with exhaustion, the swells of attachment cresting at night. On Sunday nights, I rocked my baby in a velvet green rocking chair, willing myself to put him down. *I'll give myself one hundred rocks in the chair then I have to go to bed. He'll be up every two hours through the night. I need to think clearly to write stories.*

Ninety-six, ninety-seven, ninety-eight, ninety-nine . . . I'd get to one hundred and start over. I just didn't want to put him down. It was part of my growing unease, just one of the many times I tried to ignore myself splitting in half, wanting to be in two places at once but never being fully in either.

I don't want to miss this, Jesus. I don't want to miss this gift. The thought echoed in my mind every time I dropped him off at the babysitter's house. But then I drove straight to a job I loved. The constant back and forth made me feel numb.

In journalism school I studied about how vitally important a free press is to democracy, and to me, it seemed one of the noblest careers to pursue. I woke up each morning excited to head to the office, the epicenter of information. I liked knowing things ahead of time, like a surfer riding the front of the wave before it crashed. My brain was fired up writing, thinking, and creating. I still felt butterflies every time I saw my name at the top of a story. The people I worked with were well-read, clever, and diverse. They challenged me.

I adored the adrenaline. I tracked law enforcement as they chased a fugitive in the woods, rode in a hot air balloon, rock-climbed off the faces of Mount Rushmore, knocked on dozens of doors in one of the most poverty-stricken counties in the United States, interviewed celebrities, attended funerals, sat at my desk for hours poring over school district reports and research and budgets, trying to figure out the best way to tell the story.

I remember sitting across from the mother of a seventeen-year-old boy who had hung himself two days earlier. "What do you want people to know about your son?" I asked her. I wrote fast and listened long, swallowing the lump in my throat over and over to keep from crying along with her. Strangers let me into their homes, their lives. What an honor.

And then I became a mom. And journalism, the career I had felt drawn to since high school, still felt important, but not the *most* important—until one night when I picked up Elijah from the babysitter. Leaning down to tuck him into his car seat, I breathed in the unmistakable aroma of her perfume.

He smelled like *her.* My baby smelled like another woman. And it undid me.

Weeks earlier, I had approached my boss, thinking I could negotiate my way to a compromise. *I can do this,* I reasoned. *I just need to massage my schedule until I can fit it all in. How about thirty-five hours a week? Twenty-five? How many stories can I still get done, how many moments can I not miss with this baby if I cut back to twenty-five hours?* Yet my boss needed me full-time. And there I was, torn.

It's funny how God can speak to us in the most mundane ways. His direction for my life became clear as day to me the moment

I smelled that perfume. I wanted my baby to smell like *me*. My husband might have thought I was crazy coming home that night talking about perfume. Or maybe he was relieved at my clarity. I was no longer a mother on the fence.

The numbers didn't add up on paper. We couldn't pay our bills without both of us working. Still, I went into the office the next day and told my boss I would be leaving.

I had come to the fork in the road. It's where I find so many other mothers in my community, straddling the 'in-between' while doubts and questions run laps inside their head. In that moment, I had to be honest with myself: *Has my ambition been overshadowing God's voice? How do I embrace and utilize the giftings He has given me—and be faithful to what He has called me to in this season?*

In my case, He called me to trust Him in this next season, whatever it held. It's okay to dismantle the tower in one season knowing that He may call you back to it later.

My fear, as I boxed up my desk, tucked my contact list in a folder, and closed my notebooks, was that this was it. If I left the workforce now, I would be in a vacuum, sucking the momentum right out of my sails. No one would want a washed-up writer in ten or fifteen years' time.

But God.

I let go of my death grip on my career, and sure enough, not only was I now able to stay home with my son, but God opened doors to some of the very dreams I'd had when I was back in journalism school. I remember the day I received a call from an editor in New

York City to ask if I would work on a news story as a freelancer. I got off the phone, his words still ringing in my ears and my fingers tingling with anticipation, and I couldn't believe what God had done. I had quit my full-time job, but God still cared.

From there, the world of freelance writing gradually opened up. A global news organization flew me to Alaska, Arizona, and North Dakota, let me pitch my list of dream stories, and pushed me to write better and dig deeper—all from home. It wasn't that I was such a great journalist—it was the favor of God. It was the timing of God, perfect when I was obedient.

I had stepped away from something I loved; I had dismantled a tower; I had refused to stay in the tornado I was in, and in response, He handed me the very thing my heart desired. I was stunned.

God knows the difference between the good and the great. He knows what will harm us, and what will help us thrive. He knows when we should build a tower, and when we should pack up our suitcases. And He understands that ache in our decision-making when it's something good and sweet that we have to let go of and move on from.

I still miss the newsroom. I go back and visit from time to time and thumb through the archives, my fingers smudged with ink, listen to the static of the scanner, and watch editors cut and layout the stories for tomorrow's paper. I still miss the work and the people, but when I stepped out of that building for the final time, an incredible peace came over me. The next Sunday night in the rocking chair with Elijah, I didn't have to count the rocks.

Jeremiah 29:11 says: "For I know the plans I have for you, declares the Lord, "plans to prosper you and not harm you, plans to give you a hope and a future" (NIV).

I rest in that verse. I rest in the fact that God knows what hangs in the balance when I walk in obedience to His will. I fully trust that He knows what is best for me. I never want my work desires or my goals, however noble or perfect they might seem, to crowd Him out. This is my heart: I don't want to dance around Jesus; I don't want to be distracted; I don't want to just taste what is good. Instead, I stake my claim in the fullness of the *good portion*—whatever that might be, in whatever season He has me in.

Mamas, step out of the tornado. He's waiting to meet you there.

CHAPTER SIX

FILL YOUR CUP

Most nights, my older brother and I would be found at the sink, scrubbing the evening's dishes with Dawn's soap and near-scalding water. Mom and Dad would usher us the dirty plates and double-check our work, making us go back and do it again if they found a streak of sauce on a plate or a morsel of food stuck to the tines of a fork.

Rain or shine, spaghetti or sandwiches, the two of us stood side-by-side. *I wash, you dry. Tomorrow night, you wash, I dry.*

When we moved to a larger house with a dishwasher, we didn't use it. My mom, to this day, does not use her dishwasher. She has always believed she could clean the dishes more efficiently by hand. But I also think she had something else in mind. Maybe she knew that scrubbing—of any kind—is beneficial for a kid. Maybe she understood the humility involved in scraping the greasy leftover food from someone else's plate. Maybe she sensed that my brother and I needed that little window of talk-time every night.

I thought about that this week as my kids loaded the dishwasher—the new, high-powered KitchenAid we bought on sale from Lowe's after our old one bit the dust. They can have the dishes off the table, scraped, loaded, and in the machine before we get the dressing tucked back in the fridge. I don't bemoan modern-day conveniences, but this weekend, I gave the appliance a night off and made the kids wash and dry everything by hand.

Not everything in life is meant to be fast-tracked. I need this reminder. They need this reminder. As a mom of four, I am always up for finding the most efficient way to get everything done in a day, and right now I could point you to a dozen quality books on how to be more productive, how to wring every possible minute and dollar out of your twenty-four hours.

Now, as a small business owner and a health coach, I don't dismiss the value of efficiency. But motherhood isn't a business, and it isn't just about getting things done. If it was, this journey would be much simpler. Get up. Get it done. Check it off. Good night.

Instead, mothering is all about relationships, and relationships take time. There are no hacks for this, friends, especially for how to do all this with joy. This isn't a book about helping you develop an hour-by-hour schedule to create pockets of momentary happiness with your kids. Developing deep joy during this motherhood journey that can outlast the fleeting happiness, the sorrow, and all the in-betweens, is the real intention here. You cannot rush relationship—not with God, not with your spouse, and not with your kids.

I know God's business is the heart. He cares about each morsel of our being, but He really, and I mean really, cares about that muscle beating inside our chest. *Strong's Exhaustive Concordance of the Bible* lists the primary words contained in the English Bible and I was surprised to discover the heart is cited 826 times! The point, I believe, is that He wants that muscle, which represents the very core of our being, to belong to Him.

~

I stood at the sink again a few months ago, this time with no brother alongside me to help with the dirty work. As I dipped a plate into a sink-full of sudsy water, God spoke to me, out of the blue, sure and clear.

"I don't need you to be my marketing manager."

I rested my hands in the water and stared out our back window, waiting to hear more. But that was it, not another word. I don't hear His voice like that very often. The few times I have, I feel it with my whole body, like He has struck every one of my senses.

I ruminated on it for days, rolling it around in my head, looking up Scripture, asking at times: *Was that really Him? Am I going crazy?* And finally, I settled on the fact that yes, God spoke, and yes, I heard Him.

This time, I hadn't been searching for a life-altering answer or seeking Him in the middle of a tragedy. I wasn't in prayer. I wasn't in the Word. I wasn't in conversation with a fellow believer. I was simply doing housework. And what He spoke to me seemed . . . random.

But God is never random. He never acts on the whim of an emotion—thankfully. (*Can you even imagine?*) He is certainly not a God of chaos, but of order. A God not of silliness, but substance.

Why would He have said *those words* to *me?* I have loved Jesus since I was a child, and I felt the indignation rise up in me, as though an old friend was calling me out on something.

It took me months to understand that He chose that day to speak to me in my language. It's the way we speak in my line of work—writing and communicating and storytelling—where it's my job to rally, support, and inform. God was saying to me: *I don't need you to promote me. I don't need you to run my public relations department.*

His words spoke straight to my heart.

Here's the truth: I spend so much time running around God. I talk about Him, I invite people to church, I buy my kids colorful devotionals and kneel at the bed with them at night. I tell my friends to pray. I try to persuade and guide and convince the world that He is compassionate, faithful, just, rightly jealous; that He loves them and wants to save them.

I'm doing the right things; I'm saying the right things. But eventually I slide into seasons where I'm simply running circles around Him. He knows the difference. And, in this particular season, He knew I was simply going through the motions.

That day, with my hands soaking in hot water and my mind spinning, He reminded me:

I want 'you'. I don't need you to tire yourself out, campaign for me, debate for me, convince others for me, do good works for me, or even do ministry for me. If I ask you to do all those things, it's only because I'm after one very important thing—for you to have a relationship with me. When you do this out of order, you usurp any power and authority you might have had to woo people to me. I want you to sit at my feet, to not always be about my business, but to simply be with me.

What does that look like, moms? It means, as busy as life gets, we still choose to spend one-on-one time in His Word, for His Word is bread to our souls. If you're not in the Word, you're going to starve. And can I be frank with you? There are seasons when a timely plucked verse is all you can digest and is just what you need to hang on to the end of that rope. But do not let that season continue indefinitely. You need more than a verse every couple of weeks to live on. You need a steady diet of Scripture to nourish you.

Are you intimidated by the Bible? Great, that means you're at least thinking about it. Are you reading it but confused? Great, that means you've opened it and you've started. Have you asked a silly question to a friend, or in front of the class? Great, that means you are hungry, studying with others, and humbly seeking to learn more. My point? Get over yourself, get started, and read. He will illuminate what He wants you to learn at the right moment. We just need to start somewhere, and before we know it, we will move from the milk to the solid food of His Word. Hebrews 5:13-14 assures us that: "... everyone who lives on milk is unskilled in the word of righteousness, since he is a child. But solid food is for the mature, for those who have their powers of discernment trained by constant practice to distinguish good from evil."

God doesn't need a communications team. He doesn't actually *need* anything. What He desires is committed disciples—obedient sons and daughters in relationship with Him, not because He forced it upon us, but because we tasted His goodness and we can't go back to anything less. Mamas, let's stop trying to survive all week on that meager little morsel we get on Sunday mornings, wondering why our spiritual muscles have become weakened. It's time to sit at the table and eat the meat.

$\sim$

If I close my eyes, I can picture the hands of my closest friends. I know the shape of their fingers, their fingernails, the number of diamonds in their wedding ring, their animated gestures as they tell a story.

I'm not obsessed with hands. It's just that I've spent hours in conversation with these women, watching those hands clutch coffee mugs, cup the faces of their littles, and rest next to mine on the back of a friend as we prayed during her cancer battle, asking God to please, please bring a miracle.

I've stared at their hands and I've memorized their voices day in and day out as we do the hard work of friendship. *Do I do that same genuine, hard work with God? Do I battle to know Him deeper so when I desperately need to know if it's His voice, or my flesh, or the world, or Satan whispering in my ear, I can be certain whose voice it is?*

Time breeds familiarity. How intimately are you getting to know Jesus? I need this reminder frequently. I have loved Jesus all my life, but there are seasons when I don't spend enough time *with* Him. I just spend time doing work *for* Him. There's a difference. One will eventually drain you. The other will fill your cup to the brim every time.

$\sim$

I used to play devil's advocate with people when I was younger. Scripture says that not one of us is without excuse when it comes to knowing God (Romans 1:20). But I was pretty convinced there must be someone somewhere deep in the middle of the Amazon rainforest, living among the pythons and snacking on rats, who had not heard of Jesus Christ. How could they know? And how could they call on Jesus if they simply didn't know?

My daughter asked this same question recently, and it tickled me that she mentioned someone living out in the Amazon as her example. *Like mother, like daughter.*

That verse doesn't specifically mention my 'rainforest man', but I'm pretty sure he's included. And the older I get, the more I'm realizing we actually have to go out of our way to avoid God. He's actively desiring a relationship with us, and that means He's not going to hide from us. He's everywhere.

If life is good right now, if your marriage is steady, if your kids are doing okay, if your retirement fund is growing, if your home is peaceful, God is still what you need. If you are a busy mother running the race as if your life depends on it, or if you are in a season of something heavy, God is still what you need. If you are up multiple times at night with an infant, if you are caring for an aging father, if your husband has cancer, if your teenager got into a car accident a year ago, if you walk into a workplace every morning with co-workers who thrive on drama, if you are exhausted, if you are weary, if you are at the end of your rope, God is still what you need.

You can find Him first in His Word, His teachings. Most Christian mothers in America operate in a vacuum of information. We have enough information to fill our phones, bookshelves, and conversations for multiple lifetimes yet what we often crave is the simple truth and wisdom from the one source who knows it all. Literally.

God speaks through nature, and through people. Sometimes He even speaks audibly. But guess where we can always be sure to hear His voice? In Scripture. *How many times have I danced around a decision, prayed, considered, and sought Christian wisdom from friends, but didn't take the time to cultivate and train my mind and spirit to hear His voice in the very book He wrote for me?*

Mothers, do not forsake the power of His Word. You can listen to all the podcasts, read all the self-help books, peruse the mommy blogs, go to the conferences, and spend hours at coffee and playdates, but if you are not in your Bible, you're missing out on Him—and He's missing out on you! He wants you. *All of you.*

What if we went through a season where we didn't talk with our intimate friends but instead spent all our time talking about them, about all the things we love? It would be like advertising a product we no longer know or have experience with. You cannot genuinely share what you don't know. You cannot share what you don't experience for yourself.

We let God slip to the back of our priorities, because He doesn't demand to be seen and heard. The crying infant does. The co-workers do. The needs of your home do. But the very thing we need the most, we relegate to the corner until we have time. And if we're honest with ourselves, there never really is time, is there? One day we look up, and it's gone.

If you're only just managing to read a five-minute devotional in the morning before the chaos begins, don't be discouraged. Keep going. Even a small taste creates an appetite for more of Him and, some day, with that habit locked in place, you will find yourself steeped in His Word for an hour, losing track of time because you just can't get enough.

That is my greatest hope for you. I truly believe that in every season of motherhood you can operate in joy if you are constantly in pursuit of Him. Pursue Jesus in the same way you pursue a relationship with your kids. Pursue joy the same way you pursue those sweet moments with your babies—with fervor and intention.

John 15:7 says, "If you abide in me, and my words abide in you, ask whatever you wish, and it will be done for you." When we ask for His joy, He will give it. If our heart's cry is to truly do this season of life well, we must ask for His help, and then walk it out. Make Him a priority every day, and joy will follow.

~

Our friend Freddy shared during a Bible study one night how his walk with God was a bit like living in a box. "I started out in pitch-black darkness," he said, "but every time I took another step in my relationship with God, it was as though another hole was punched into that box."

As he spoke, I imagined sitting in that dark box—comfortable, content, unknowing. And then a speck of light breaks in as God reveals something of Himself. I wondered, *at what point would there be so many holes that the cardboard became flimsy, the sides started caving in, and you shake free of the sagging, unstable box you have been living in?*

As I write, the pandemic is winding down. It served as a timely catalyst to adjust our schedules and realign our priorities. Yet still I hear Him loud and clear: *I am God. Sit with me. Listen to me. Hear me, truly hear me. And then, only then, will you be equipped to go out into the world and be my hands and feet.*

In his book, *Mere Discipleship: Radical Christianity in a Rebellious World*, theologian Lee Camp writes:

> "Jesus of Nazareth always comes asking disciples to follow him—not merely 'accept him,' not merely 'believe in him,' not merely 'worship him,' but to follow him: one either follows Christ, or one does not. There is no compartmentalization of the faith, no realm, no sphere, no business, no politic in which the lordship of Christ will be excluded. We either make him Lord of all lords, or we deny him as Lord of any."

So many of us simply want Jesus to be the icing on the cake. We don't want to reorder our lives, to sacrifice too much, to shake things up, to challenge the status quo. We don't want to lay down our life.

We just want to hold the cake and plop Jesus on the top. Or if we want a little more substance, we add Him in like another ingredient, along with the eggs and vanilla. We want Him in the mix, enhancing our life. But, at the end of the day, He's just one ingredient of many.

But Jesus isn't the icing, or an optional ingredient. He's inextricably in the mix, in every decision, in every consideration. And when we surrender ourselves to that truth—when we fully engage in relationship with Him, opening our hands and giving Him everything—that is when we can truly mother with joy.

Everything else is just icing.

CHAPTER SEVEN

ONE THING

It was manic, getting the kids to school each morning. I was in a season with four littles, and ushering all of them out the door took strategy, manpower, and grace. By the time I'd strapped all the kids into their car seats and slid into the front seat of my van, my heart was pounding, my makeup (if I had any on) was smudged, and I always seemed to have forgotten something that required a mad dash back into the house. It seemed no matter how early I got up, we always arrived late.

Even so, I did one thing every morning. Before we left the house I would physically drop to the floor—just long enough for my knees to tap the ground—and ask the Holy Spirit to fill me. That was it: I'd pause just long enough to pray, "Holy Spirit, please, please fill me," and then I'd be up and running again. I still do it sometimes, even though life is calmer now.

Odd? Yes. But my 'knee tap' is more than a quirky way to redirect my thoughts. It is a conscious decision to plug into Him when things feel hurried, stressful, or out of control. And in that season,

I needed to perform that physical act, even just for a few seconds, to rein in and refocus my mind. *I'm headed out of the house. I have four little human beings who need me to be present. Please God, meet me in this craziness, in this rush.*

We overcomplicate heart and head matters sometimes. Mama, if you are rooted in Christ, then you have a Helper—you are not doing this alone. The Holy Spirit is *the* Helper, and when you are struggling, or at the end of your rope, or stressed out with sweat on your brow, the Holy Spirit is better than any yoga session, nanny, housecleaner, or vacation. Living a Spirit-filled life is not a mystery; it's not based on some magical formula, and it's not simply a lofty aspiration for mature Christians. The fruits of the Spirit—love, joy, peace, patience, kindness, goodness, faithfulness, gentleness, and self-control—can be yours. In the midst of your overwhelm, you can call on Him to overwhelm you with His joy, and to manifest every one of these gifts in your life. It will change the way you mother your kids. It will change the course of your days.

∼

When one of the neighborhood kids told my son last week that I was "one of the nice moms," I was pleasantly surprised—especially coming from this particular middle-schooler, whom I had corrected just the week before.

But cultivating a spirit of joy in your home isn't about being the fun mom, or the nice mom, or the pretty mom. It's about setting boundaries in love and overflowing in the fruits of the Spirit as we consistently discipline our children.

Do not count on a steady stream of 'good days' to cultivate a spirit of joy. It will not be good every day. It might not be good for weeks or even months. How do you exercise that muscle—the one that helps us default to His goodness, His patience, His endurance—when you just want to yell, or cry, or sit down and quit this whole motherhood thing? You do it *consistently*, even when it's hard, that's how. It's like training any other muscle.

There's no fake it 'til you make it in the business of mothering with joy. Getting by until you get it figured out is great advice for taking a dance class, but not for this. There are no do-overs with this.

You can fake happiness, but you can't fake joy. And the single greatest factor in cultivating the way you mother with joy is your relationship with Jesus. In Psalm 1 we are promised that if we delight in the law of the Lord, meditating on it day and night, we will be filled with joy and prosper, because we will be bearing fruit in each of life's seasons. Our children must be the caretaker of their own heart, but as a mom pursuing joy, I am one of their single greatest influences, and I don't want to lead them astray.

Paul writes in 2 Corinthians 6:10: "Our hearts ache, but we always have joy. We are poor, but we give spiritual riches to others. We own nothing, and yet we have everything" (NLT). In Romans 12:12, he encourages us to "be joyful in hope, patient in affliction, faithful in prayer" (NIV).

I regularly ask God for provision, for freedom from bondage, for wisdom, for safety, for healing, for work and for rest, so why would I not also ask for His joy? If I'm not asking, I'm trying to do it in my own strength.

Joy is a mindset, a habit, a muscle. Nehemiah 8:10 says that the joy of the Lord is my strength. It's a supernatural gifting that is at the core of who God is. I cannot do this motherhood journey without it.

Let's ask, and then listen. We have pockets of time during our day which we tend to fill with one voice or another—a podcast, worship music, a call to a friend. They are all good things. But do we make room for silence so we can hear Him speak? Just Him? Just His voice?

It's an intentional decision to listen for His voice. God absolutely does speak, direct and guide us through other people, but we don't always need an intercessor. Ask yourself, are you leaving space for Him to speak directly to you? Or, even after consuming all the books, podcasts, commentaries and magazines, and hearing from radio personalities, preachers and theologians, are you still distracted and spiritually starving?

When I became a mom, I didn't realize the number of additional influences that would enter my sphere and crowd out the voice of God. I listened to the doctor, my friends, Google, grandparents, all the experts. There are so many experts.

In a twenty-four-hour day, the average person hears between 20,000 and 30,000 words. Even if we disagree with them or don't allow them to stick, they still subconsciously become a part of us and shape how we think. The voices you hear influence you. Plain and simple.

What voices do you need to limit or silence? Are you speaking a lifegiving narrative over yourself? Your words have the power to encourage, motivate, remind, refresh, and offer to you and others a mindset based on truth.

This is not simply an exercise in positive self-talk. You're calling on the power of the Holy Spirit, who can, quite literally do anything. When I call on His name, I'm doing two things. I'm first training my mind and body in the habit of calling on Him. Second, I'm stepping aside, getting out of His way, and letting His Spirit and gifts flow.

In Matthew 7:7 we read, "Ask, and it will be given to you; seek, and you will find; knock, and it will be opened to you." If you need something, call on the name of Jesus—out loud. If I need strength, joy, patience, self-control, I ask for it with bold humility. I speak it out loud. Whatever I need in that moment, I ask for it. I don't care who hears. My kids are used to me praying over them throughout the day, rebuking the enemy, adjusting my attitude with my words.

There's plenty the Holy Spirit is doing in my head and my heart I don't share, but I'm not ashamed to call on His name—out loud. It's okay for my kids to know that I am not doing this on my own. In fact, I desperately want them to hear me turning to Christ when I need His help.

Recently, my kids flitted from room to room as we finished chores, and I overheard them arguing about a pack of gum. Yes, a pack of gum. I know you've been there. One minute we're scrubbing the sticky off the kitchen floor, and the next thing I know, we're engaged in an all-out battle of wills. I can feel the heat rising in my face, my raw flesh rubbing up against the Holy Spirit. *I could yell. I really could yell right now, and I think it would feel good.*

But I don't yell, because as I'm teaching my kids, what feels good in the moment isn't a good barometer for decision-making. So, I harness my tongue, redirect the conversation, dole out consequences, and reset the atmosphere.

I don't need to throw myself a pity party because motherhood is hard some days. Instead, I need to ask the Holy Spirit for help. In his letter to the Philippians, Paul was pretty clear about how believers move forward in faith: *Do all things without grumbling or disputing . . . rejoice in the Lord . . . forget what lies behind and reach forward to what lies ahead . . . press on toward the goal . . . rejoice in the Lord always.* It's all included in the daily work of motherhood.

James writes that we should count it *all joy* when we meet trials of various kinds (James 1:2). This joy also helped Jesus endure the cross. In Scripture we read that He, "for the joy that was set before him endured the cross, despising the shame, and is seated at the right hand of the throne of God" (Hebrews 12:2).

Mamas, I need to hear this as much as you: quit your whining. He prepared you for this. He continues to prepare you. He will always prepare you.

A friend once told me that God loves us and created us, but He is not to be bothered with the mundane tasks and trials of daily life. "God didn't create us to babysit us," he told me.

I think my friend's heart was in the right place. God did create us, and He gave us stewardship over the details. But I couldn't disagree more with the rest of it. Our God is a God of intricate design, a master storyteller, a genius weaver of plots and love lines. By recognizing this, I'm not trying to bring God down to my level in a power play—I'm recognizing His sovereignty, that He is the One who brings redemption and victory. God is neither a puppet master hovering over the stage of our life, pulling and pushing the ropes of a wooden doll to make legs and arms move, nor a God who spoke us into existence then left on vacation.

He's here. And He cares about the details. Look at these verses from Scripture:

"The Lord directs the steps of the godly. He delights in every detail of their lives" (Psalm 37:23 NLT).

"We can make our plans, but the Lord determines our steps" (Proverbs 16:9 NLT).

"Are not five sparrows sold for two pennies? And not one of them is forgotten before God. Why, even the hairs of your head are all numbered. Fear not: you are of more value than many sparrows" (Luke 12:6-7).

If God is indeed watching us from His lofty lifeguard post instead of being down in the pool with us, how does He know the number of hairs on our head, and why does He wrestle with Jacob or stand in the fire with Daniel? He's God Almighty, majestic, holy . . . and He's in the muck *with* us, fighting for our hearts.

God is with us.

Let that truth seep into your soul. There is never a moment that He turns a blind eye. And in return, we have the freedom to be in relationship with Him. It's much like the way we raise our children—not hovering or trying to force a relationship, but always there, always loving, allowing them the space and time they need to be themselves. I love my kids, therefore I am invested in the details of their lives—not to micromanage, but to enjoy.

Without Jesus, I would be an overly scheduled, cranky hot mess who yells a lot. So, I daily ask Him to fill my cup, to set my default to joy. I certainly don't want my cup filled with more of *me*—my tendencies, my weaknesses, my agitations, my thought processes— all of which lead me to places He doesn't want me to go.

Mamas, let's not allow the noise of the world to crowd out God's overflow of joy. Let's consistently call on the name of the One who can help us. Let's seek His voice, so we can be moms who shepherd our children in a way that marks us as different and leads other people to Christ.

CHAPTER EIGHT

WASH FEET

The summer I managed to kick off an ongoing neighborhood war began innocently enough. To be fair, they started off in swimsuits. Then my toddlers got naked.

With three kids under the age of six, and nine months pregnant with my fourth, I was swollen, achy, ready. During the sweltering month of July I fluctuated between the sweet anticipation of our final baby and complete exhaustion—little sleep, a thirty-eight-pound weight gain, and feet so swollen it hurt to slip on sandals.

My husband took our eldest son on their annual week-long fishing trip, and I spent much of it on the front porch eating popsicles, letting my two youngest run in the sprinklers, and reading up on how to induce labor.

That week I had a burst of energy—not to *do* more necessarily, but to create some Pinterest-worthy memories for my kiddos. Mommy-guilt settled into my bones—my kids were enduring the summer with a mom who wanted to do little more than watch the action from the comfort of a recliner.

So, out came the swimsuits, the water hose, and the shaving cream. I handed each of my kids a can and let them spray to their heart's content. It was glorious. They spent an entire hour swiping the foam across the ground, the swimming pool, the side of the house, and their bodies. Then they ran to the faucet, rinsed it off, and started all over.

It checked off all the 'good mommy' points: educational, sensory-laden, and creative. I was proud. I was relaxed.

A little too relaxed.

Lathered in shaving cream, my two-year-old, who was potty training and often stripped out of his clothes to pee, suddenly slipped off his trunks and bolted around the lawn. My four-year-old daughter soon followed suit.

I get it. We're training them up to be modest, sexual predators do exist, and as a general rule, humans wear clothes. But that summer it just all went by the wayside. And, I'll be frank here, this mama didn't care.

Apparently, someone else did. One of our neighbors, who, unbeknownst to me had been harboring a distaste for our family during the preceding six months (even when my kids were fully clothed), started yelling before she had even crossed the street, then got to our front porch and waved her finger in my face. Furious my kids had been naked, she proceeded to vent at me. She wanted to move; we were running a nudist colony; she was tired of us, and we were upsetting all the other neighbors. (I'm sparing you the colorful language.)

My kids froze, and though my heart thumped solidly against my ribcage, I stayed completely calm. I tried to interject, all of it apologies. "You're right. I am so sorry. I understand. Please forgive us. We'll do better."

She wasn't having it. She just kept yelling and yelling and yelling. I sat and listened, stunned and humiliated. I felt terrible.

When she finally walked back to her house, I pulled the kids inside, my stomach in knots. My husband and I talked it over that night. Our kids were fully clothed while outside from that day forward. We sat them down, explained that we had messed up, and reinforced the rules. We talked about anger, about self-control, about forgiveness.

I sent handwritten apology notes to every neighbor in our cul-de-sac, asking for forgiveness and telling them we would be better neighbors. They told me they loved our kids running in the yard and enjoyed the energy and life they brought to the neighborhood, which brought relief but never fully annulled the worry I now harbored about how others viewed our family or my parenting.

Despite my best efforts, our neighbor is still mad. In response to the apology note, she reminded me (with a profanity-laced declaration from her front porch) that it is a federal offense to put something in someone's mailbox.

A month after her outburst, while walking past our neighbor's front yard with our six-day-old baby strapped to my chest, her husband called out to congratulate us on our new addition to the family. Quickly she appeared behind him, berating him for talking with us and yelling about the things she hates about our family as we walked away.

It breaks my heart each time we have these interactions, not just because she doesn't like us, but because I can't make it right. Sometimes you mess up, and even with the best of intentions, people can't find it in their heart to forgive.

Our relationship has deteriorated since; the incidents involving her now number a long list. Last summer, I felt that familiar fear creeping into my thoughts. *What if she does something to one of the kids? What if she always lives here and I have to constantly worry about something bad happening?*

So, that night, I padded out on to our driveway in my socks long after the sun had slid behind the hill. It was the hour just past twilight when a slow hush envelops our neighborhood, the energy of the day tucked away behind drawn shades.

I strode to the center of our cul-de-sac, faced our house, and stared at the outline of the blue construction heart taped to the front window, put up during the Covid-19 pandemic and now illuminated by the living room lamp. In the darkness around me, that heart seemed to glow.

I felt a familiar feeling rising up in me—not that of a mama bear, but a warrior. If I was in the midst of a spiritual battle here, I knew what I needed to do. I wrapped my robe tighter around my waist, closed my eyes, and raised my hands toward our house.

Then I prayed. I prayed over the property line around our house. I prayed over the doors, the driveway, the rooms in which our babies slept, our bedroom, the yard.

And then I turned and faced her house, and I did the same. I prayed over the bills in her mailbox, the deck where they grill, their new puppy, the front door, and her vehicle. Then I prayed over her mind, her heart, her emotions, her tongue, her past, her marriage, and the people at her job.

Someone might have peeked out their front window at that moment and caught a glimpse of me in my pajamas, arms raised, eyes closed, standing in the gap for my family and for this neighbor. They might have thought I was crazy, and that's okay.

Peace—His peace—lodged in my heart that night.

That neighbor is across the street from us for a reason. I believe it. I am to behave differently than the rest of the world in how I respond to her. If she can't see the joy in me, that's a problem. It's time, not to fear, but to dig deep and find compassion for this woman, to actively pray for her even when the mama bear in me wants to rise up and meet her in the middle of the road.

The following week, I pulled into our cul-de-sac, and there was her green garbage bin tipped over, the contents blowing across her yard.

"Go pick it all up," the Holy Spirit whispered.

What? Are you serious? But she's mean. I prayed over her. I'm good.

"The garbage, go get it."

No way. I'm not stepping foot on her property. She hates our family. She makes my blood boil. She deserves a little garbage blowing around her yard.

"The time is now."

I don't always catch those whispers from the Holy Spirit: that tingle in your fingertips to give to that homeless man even as your brain is running through scenarios of why he might not have a job, that tightening of your stomach when you're about to blurt something out and His presence thankfully shuts your mouth.

Sometimes, I miss the window—I either choose to ignore it or I wait too long and miss it. Yet the more deeply rooted I am in Christ, the more aware I am of these divine moments. I know now it's better to just move, right when He asks. Whatever God is orchestrating—a simple meal for a hungry man on the street, a shield of protection for the tender heart of a co-worker when my words would have cut them deep—is really about my obedience. It's about my heart. *Am I willing to lay down my pride, or whatever fleshly desire I am tempted by, and simply move?*

I pulled up next to her driveway and said a silent prayer that some alarm wouldn't immediately sound. I darted from one piece of garbage to the next, the wind whipping my hair into my eyes and stinging my cheeks. I plucked sticky leftovers, wet bottles, and crumpled papers back into the bin and wrestled to get it upright and back on to the road—this time facing a different direction in the hopes it wouldn't fall over again.

When I got back into the car, my heart raced but I felt awash with relief. Praise the Lord she hadn't come storming out her front door. *What would I have said?*

I recognize God's hand in it all. Since that first summer, our neighbor has cussed, glared, flipped off, screamed, and otherwise made it clear that she is not a fan of me. There have been many days of battling my flesh—biting my tongue, not screaming back, figuring out how to navigate safety for my family in hostile situations.

Yet I also noticed my heart growing cold toward her. And God, our all-knowing Creator who also fashioned my neighbor's life, knew I could not demonstrate His love well while also fearing this woman. He needed me humble and available, living proof that the fruits of the Spirit can thrive even in untenable conditions. I could not genuinely demonstrate to my kids, who now also harbored fear and distrust of her, to call on the name of Jesus with authority when they were scared or angry in a confrontation with her, if I first didn't lead by example.

We are not the only family with kids in our neighborhood, and the space around our home often pulses with energy—nerf gun wars, water balloons, basketball, the trampoline, bikes . . . so many bikes. The kids run from house to house; they hang out in the fort in our backyard which is old and well-loved and leaning a little too much to the side. I listen to their conversations when they come through the back door, sweat-streaked and smelling of dirt, popping apple slices into open mouths. I hear them refer to our neighbor as "the mean lady".

So, I stop them, and I remind them of her name. I remind them that she is a mom too, that she is married, that she puts lights on her house at Christmas just like us. I want them to see her, really see her—not the caricature they have created of her in their mind. I want them to see what it looks like when we don't write people off—even when they mess up.

Yes, she has been a thorn in my side. But God breathed life into her, and if she does not know Jesus or has turned from Him, we want to be the neon sign pointing back to Him. Nothing more. Nothing less.

God will deal with her heart, I tell them, so let's let Him deal with ours, too.

~

I read as many of Dietrich Bonhoeffer's writings as I can. I love to study his perspective and the arc of his story. Maybe it's because he wasn't a woman, or a mom, and his life as a theologian during the rise of Hitler is about as far from mine as it can get. But the way he writes about the pure, insatiable way we are to pursue Christ strikes a chord in my heart like no other author. *Love Jesus unapologetically, even to the detriment of luxury or comfort, even to death.* That was the anthem of Bonhoeffer's life.

In one of my favorite books of his, Bonhoeffer reminds us that Jesus Christ lived in the midst of His enemies:

"At the end, all his disciples deserted him," he writes. "On the Cross he was utterly alone, surrounded by evildoers and mockers. For this cause he had come, to bring peace to the enemies of God. So the Christian, too, belongs not in the seclusion of a cloistered life but in the thick of foes."

He goes on to quote Luther:

"The kingdom is to be in the midst of your enemies. And he who will not suffer this does not want to be of the Kingdom of Christ; he wants to be among friends, to sit among roses and lilies, not with the bad people but the devout people. O you blasphemers and betrayers of Christ! If Christ had done what you are doing who would ever have been spared."[1]

Am I so fragile a believer that I can't handle the spiritual warfare in my own cul-de-sac? My desire is to be confident enough in my relationship with Jesus that I can strap on my armor and leave the walls of my castle to face the world.

Jesus modeled this with excellence. How easy it would have been for Him to surround Himself with his twelve-pack of disciples, preach at will, fish for fun, and enjoy a lot of free late-night dinners.

But He didn't. He got His hands dirty. He set his priorities from the get-go: spend time alone with God, build a tight-knit circle of friends, then devote the rest of His energy outward—to the world. He never avoided confrontation but brought peace to it. He never sold out, but masterfully redirected conversations and confusion back to truth. He never ran from ugliness, the broken, the messy, or the yuck, but redeemed it.

---

1   Life Together: The Classic Exploration of Christian Community

Remember Judas, the man who betrayed Him? Judas operated from inside Jesus' very own circle of friends, His own tribe. Yet Jesus spoke truth to His friend, kept him at His side, and then, even with the foresight of his betrayal, broke bread with Judas and washed his feet. We read,

> *"The evening meal was in progress, and the devil had already prompted Judas, the son of Simon Iscariot, to betray Jesus. Jesus knew that the Father had put all things under his power, and that he had come from God and was returning to God . . . he poured water into a basin and began to wash his disciples' feet."*
> *(John 13:2-5 NIV)*

Jesus had come from God and was returning to God.

In the same way, I know who I belong to, who I came from, and where I'm going. Is that assurance, that delight in knowing Him, enough to get me through the yuck? *It is. Is it enough to wash the feet of my neighbor when He calls me to it? It is.*

The trendy thing right now is to "find your tribe". Find your people. Stick with them. Pour into them. I get it—there are deep, soul-healing, life-altering friendships to be found, and we'll talk more about that later. I have found my people, and they have been a lifeline for me. But if we insulate ourselves from the world by living inside our tribe, if we only deeply discuss life with people who agree with us, if we only serve and forgive and love our inner circle, we're really no better than the Pharisees.

Hear me out: I am not talking about letting someone abuse you or walk all over you. I'm asking you to let God speak wisdom into every encounter and confrontation in spite of the emotions that may be pulsing through your veins.

We build the Kingdom of Jesus not by hiding behind walls and volleying attacks back at whoever has injured us. Instead, we get bold. We get out of our comfort zone. We live with joy because that's exactly the opposite of what the world does. If there's something our neighborhoods are longing to see right now, it's not vengeance; it's the sweet aroma of Christ. It's the radical joy of Jesus.

Moms, your children absorb a profound lesson when you do the right thing, the uncomfortable thing. You can rub shoulders with someone who believes different things than you. You can live next to someone who spews hatred every day and it need not rock you to your core. It can refine you, steel you for doing harder things later.

My kids, who are now always fully clothed, witness the way our neighbor consistently lobs assaults at our family. They are oftentimes the target, and if I ever needed to physically stand between her and them, there's no question where I would be.

But in the meantime, I'm doing the spiritual battling, and in turn, teaching *them* to do the spiritual battling—the hard work that wins the real war. I want my kids to continually witness me reaching deep into that fountain of joy in the face of adversity, even in the little things, and to know that they can too.

So, we pray. We let our home glow. We pick up garbage. And we wash feet.

CHAPTER NINE

GATHER

I don't like coffee. I like the idea of coffee, but not the actual taste of coffee. My husband brews a pot in the morning, and the house fills with the aroma of freshly-ground hazelnut coffee beans. He drinks it black, the steam rising to his bearded face, and I pour myself a cup and anticipate loving it the way everyone else does.

And then I taste it, and I cannot fathom how people like this liquid— pressed, ground, steamed from beans, soaked in hot water, and then poured into whatever worn homemade mug from college or trendy Yeti is resting in the cupboard. And those friends who drink their coffee straight from the pot, just black and hot? Mind boggling. And yet, I like what coffee has done in my life. It's a cup of warmth in more ways than one, a staple that seems to cross every global culture and draw people together.

I was a first-time mom when my friend Deanna gathered a few of us together for a weekly study at her house, just coffee and moms, Bibles and babies. I had just quit my job, and pockets of time opened.

We started as strangers and acquaintances, and our initial plan was to meet for a year. A new mom herself, Deanna craved what I longed for as well—consistent fellowship and deeper friendships. A wisdom ran beneath the invitation. She knew God had called us to not forsake coming together, even in the season of littles.

Sitting on her living room floor at that first gathering, I didn't know this was the start of something bigger. God was laying the groundwork for a network of life-giving friendship, discipleship and mentorship He knew I desperately needed in this season of life.

That same core group continued meeting year after year. We met when we felt rested and encouraged, when we were falling more in love with our spouse, when we got the job, when we came back refreshed from vacation. And we didn't give up meeting when we were exhausted, when our bellies were swollen with babies, when we miscarried and lost mamas to cancer, when things got rocky at home and finances were paycheck to paycheck.

There were times when it was a hard season for someone, yet the person next to them was in a season of abundance and growth—or heading downhill to the valley. And that was good and sweet, because we are never all resting in the valley together or trudging up the mountain at the same time. This rubbing of our shoulders as we move through differing vantage points creates the wisdom and the will to keep moving forward.

Our group navigated life together, and though the roots started small and flimsy—our friendships woven together by our similar faith and parenting—those roots took hold as we huddled in prayer, engaged in debate, wept over loss, and laughed—really laughed.

A couple of months after I had my third baby, I woke up one morning disheveled and worn out. This baby didn't sleep for very long, ever. He stayed up on and off through the night, nursing, crying, fussing, and then napped very little during the day. Sleep deprivation proved to be one of the cruelest mental battles I faced.

I still got in the car that morning, bleary-eyed and shaky, and drove across town to my friend's house for Bible study. I sat cross-legged on the living room floor, let one of my friends take the infant from my arms, and took a deep breath to keep from crying. I felt an abyss opening beneath me, as if I were sinking beneath the weight of a heavy, unbearable kind of tiredness I had never experienced before. A deep-seated, eyes burning, body aching exhaustion.

I poured an inch of coffee into a mug, filled the rest with milk and dollops of creamer, and I didn't say much that day. I just sat on the floor and listened. I wanted nothing more than to curl up in my bed and sleep for hours, for days. I craved sleep more than anything. But something happened that morning that gave me a new breath, a small respite from the exhaustion.

As I listened to their stories intermingle with God's Word, the bubbling of conversation soft and steady, I felt my shoulders loosen, the fog lifting. Then, something wonderful happened. I looked across the room at Jonah, this new little life we had been gifted, and felt a subtle but certain contentment. This was how God had created a space of rest for me. Right here, in a roomful of people. *How was that possible?*

This is the beautiful, transformative work of friendship. This is what can happen in genuine community, when you put in the time and work and allow the Holy Spirit to move. When you show up. With the groundwork laid, there is a place of rest, a pocket in the world where you are held in high esteem, safe, loved, and in the company of others with no agenda.

Another thing can happen in this kind of circle—if you let it. Your mind informs your heart, and in turn, your heart informs your mind: *God can move here, I can learn here. Let's let the walls down, let my guards down.*

I laid down my pride about my faith, my marriage, my theology, my motherhood. I earnestly listened and asked questions, took notes, and sought the influence of the Holy Spirit in a deeper way than I had before. And growth happened.

Author Donald Miller wrote in *Blue Like Jazz:* "God risked Himself on me. I will risk myself on you. And together, we will learn to love, and perhaps then, and only then, understand this gravity that drew Him, unto us." That risk is at the heart of relationship. You have to put something of yourself on the line.

We have new and expecting mamas in our church now, and I see that sweet mixture of elation and worry. They cup a hand on their swollen belly and it almost takes my breath away, the deep, poignant way their life is about to change. I want desperately to pull them aside, take them by the hand and tell them, "You will survive the nights; no, you don't need a baby wipe warmer; stick close to your husband, you're in this together."

I especially want to remind them how deeply valuable and vital it is to find friendship. Find Christ-seeking friends who will show up, link arms with you, and commit to navigating life together. Pray for it, seek it out, be that kind of friend, and when you find it, dig in, invest, and don't let it go.

One of the most vulnerable aspects of friendship is getting close enough to let another woman speak into your mothering journey. We all need friends who will not only battle with us in prayer but hold us up when this mission seems insurmountable, who will celebrate our victories but speak truth when we're off track, who will point out the blind spots and call us to do better. These friendships are more than a safety net; they become part of the fabric of who we are. It matters in every season of life, and it really matters during motherhood.

C.S. Lewis said in *The Four Loves*: "To love at all is to be vulnerable . . . if you want to make sure of keeping it intact you must give it to no one, not even an animal. Wrap it carefully with hobbies and little luxuries; avoid all entanglements. Lock it safe in the casket or coffin, safe, dark, motionless, airless, it will change. It will not be broken; it will become unbreakable, impenetrable, irredeemable. To love is to be vulnerable."

Sometimes a friendship is so natural, like sliding your hand into a well-fitting glove. Our friends Freddy and Leslee took a theology college course with us before we became parents. A month into the class, they invited us to Leslee's grandparents' farm for the weekend a few hours away. We spent our days pheasant hunting, taste-testing her grandma's beef roast, weaving in and out of barns and Aspen trees. It was a peek into a life with kids (they already had three boys), and a chance to witness the minutia of life with littles. That trip opened the gates to a deep friendship and became a pivot point in our family's life—on the ride home, we decided we were ready to have kids.

It's been almost fifteen years, our friendship now refined by the hours and hours of our families walking alongside each other—babysitting, late night cake-decorating, packing and moving homes, weekends at the lake, cliff jumping. We have been honest with each other, confessed our sins, battled together in prayer, watched and learned from each other's mistakes, and cheered each other on from a place of truly wanting the best for one another. One of their teenage sons wrote me a birthday note last year that said I felt like another mom.

These friendships are familial, safe, loyal. We all need those kind of friends—those we allow behind the curtain to see the parts of us still under construction, the parts we like to hide.

I am grateful for the friends who knew me growing up and have continued to weave threads of trust and time into our relationship despite the miles apart and the near-impossible task it seems to carve out the time to connect.

This fall I traveled home for my friend Alison's fortieth birthday celebration. In preschool we ate sweet tart candies beneath the swooping branches of her backyard willow tree and called boys from the landline phone in her attic in middle school. In high school, Tarrin moved to our hometown, and the three of us formed a triad of friendship that helped me navigate my teenage years with a grace and maturity I would not have garnered on my own.

I called Tarrin last night, in between the dinner and baths—just to hear her voice. I can close my eyes and it's as comfortable as it was twenty-five years ago. It was her voice next to me as I drove my first car, spent hours memorizing biology facts, dreamt of college—that comforted me, with a sure slip of her arm around my shoulder as I wept over my parents, that *it will be okay.*

I am astonished at how, living in three different states with twelve children between us, the three of us still manage to create space for each other—a weekend trip to Seattle to peruse Pike's Place Market, or a hike at Red Rocks Amphitheater in Colorado. By the time I'm home, my voice is a whisper, having talked and laughed late into the night, desperately trying to soak up every piece of advice, memorizing the way they look and smile and hug because I just don't know when I'll get to be with them again.

How sweet and strange it is to watch them wrap their arms around their own daughters now. I want to pull those girls aside, whisper in their ears amusing stories about their mom's teenage years. But mostly, I want to tell them their mom was a lifeline, and still is, and that our time together colors so many areas of my life.

Each of these friendships—the deep, lifelong friendships, the new friendships, and the ones on the periphery—have changed the way I mother my kids. They fill a need inside me to serve and love and pour into relationships outside my family, and to be influenced by others in a way that makes me want to genuinely try harder.

It takes hard work and trust and prayer to keep real friendship going, much like our relationship with Christ. And much like our relationship with Christ, the return on our investment is always sweeter and fuller than we expected.

∽

Today, we met around Kristen's kitchen table and doled out tacos and watermelon and homemade guacamole and talked for hours. There's a different level of vulnerability that happens when you meet in someone's home. It's been a decade now, and though the cadence of our conversation is familiar, the topics have changed. It's the same ebb and flow of conversation—schedules, challenges, what made us laugh that week—but the undercurrent is always more serious. *Are we stewarding our children well?*

That's what I love about continuing to invest in this close-knit circle. We get to heart matters. Some days it would be easier to do motherhood in a vacuum, far away from the prying eyes of others. I might mess up; I might do this wrong; my kids aren't perfect, and it would just be easier if I did this alone. Yet I push back against that faulty thinking because isolation does little for the soul and much less for parenting.

I also push back against the contamination of comparison and jealousy and gossip which claw at each of our friendships if we let it, degrading the roots of our relationships. Relationships are not a chess game, yet sometimes we try to make them so. We wait and see how someone will react or respond, and that determines how we plan our next move. If we are always strategizing, however, we have stifled our ability to open our heart to simply move when He says move.

If we live life like a game, we limit our ability to be obedient to God's direction regardless of what the other person does or says. Moreover, it traps us in a negative thought cycle, leaving us incapable of thinking about anything except the 'game' we're playing. It's not a healthy place to be.

When I asked God to help me see each woman around me as a beautiful creation of His, not a representation of everything I am not—a person to be envied or 'one-upping'—I let go of comparing.

I don't want to compete with you; I want to cheer you on to wherever God is leading you. So, when it comes to comparing what kind of mom I am, what kind of house we're running, what kind of kids we are raising, I have to rebuke that spirit of comparison in Jesus' name and lay down my pride. Every time.

I just turned forty, and I want to skip the fluff. I want to find the balance between doing life together and not getting caught up in the things that are not eternal. I started health coaching three years ago, and the more I shared my journey with others, the more I realized I don't have to be perfect; I just have to be willing.

The women I minister to need more than recipes and gift bags and pats on the back. I've stood next to these women for years and had no idea they were in the throes of addiction or grieving an abortion from two decades ago or scratching and clawing their way back to a relationship with an estranged son or daughter.

I am a lover of people and community and conversation. I love gatherings and potlucks and fundraisers—of which there have been plenty. But what my heart really aches for are nitty-gritty, bare your soul, in-it-to-win-it, relational discipleship kind of friendships.

I took a ministry leadership survey a couple of years ago and wasn't surprised that I scored an 8 for *concern for people*, and a 2 for *concern for productivity*. I genuinely care about people, and I relate to people in a way that can overshadow my productivity.

Relationships can't be measured in a tangible way. You walk away from the conversation, your hands still jittery from the caffeine, and you can't check anything off the to-do list. But make no mistake, there was a shifting in your soul, a subtle carving of your pride, a pruning of your attitude, or the blossoming of your confidence. Work was done. We just can't always see it.

Mamas, do not underestimate the impact of the people in your circle. Do not undervalue a friend who loves you enough to correct you. It hurts to listen to a gentle rebuke and it may be hard to receive it with care and due diligence, but the results are most often deeply sweet and confirming.

I came across a photograph last week of two infant boys propped on a sofa, both of them wide-eyed and rosy-cheeked. It's Deanna's son Braysin and my son Elijah, born just months apart. This year, I snapped a picture after their first middle school basketball season game, fresh off the court, sweaty, tussled hair, arms slung over each other's shoulders. We feel so far from that infant photo.

They now stand on the cusp of their teenage years and I know the terrain is different from here on out—cell phones and curfews, part-time jobs and biology. But there's even more on the line—how do we train them up in righteousness? How do we help these boys become warriors for Jesus? How do we help teach them to become men who can lead and love?

Standing in the gym, I link arms with Deanna, her face flush with the same pride and emotion I feel as we witness another milestone and I'm overcome by God's perfect timing. Elijah has a friend who's been there since day one, and I've got another mama in the trenches with me, cheering on and praying over my babies. How can that not make me want to weep with gratitude?

We all need those people with whom we can let our guard down instead of worrying they won't like what they see—a space where we allow the Holy Spirit to reveal things about ourselves. Friend, this is hard work. It doesn't come naturally. Sure, the social part might come naturally, but not the prying open of your mind and heart.

It took extended time with my friends to really voice what specific sin I was struggling with in my life or be able to share with raw emotion when my child had done something wrong or hurt someone and I needed guidance. Our walk with God is always personal, but it's not always private. We were made to do life together. Sometimes that looks like a roomful of people. Other times it's a long-distance phone call, a hike, or sitting together on the floor of your living room with babies crawling in and out of your lap. Yet wherever or however you are tying your heart to others, do not forsake it during this season of motherhood. When Jesus said, "Where two or three are gathered in my name, there am I among them" (Matthew 18:20), He was saying something very clear, something life-defining to us all: *Gather.*

CHAPTER TEN

CARVED TO FIT

My husband keeps a picture of the two of us on his dresser. It was taken on my mom's porch just a couple of weeks after our first baby arrived. We're standing there, parenthood still so fresh. He's bearded, young and proud, our firstborn swaddled in his arms, and I'm tucked in at his side, my face swollen, tired, grinning. In both our eyes there's a sure look of contentment, like we have softly landed someplace we always wanted to go.

We keep that picture where we see it every day to remind us how far we've come and where we're going, much as Moses placed markers along the route from Egypt to the Promised Land signifying the times when manna appeared or when God gave His people a specific revelation. That framed picture is a small vestige of the past—the 'old us' talking to the 'new us'—*you have been here before, you can do it again, God's got this.* It's a reminder that in parenthood or marriage you never really fully arrive, you just keep going. How many times can we remind ourselves of His faithfulness, of His promises fulfilled? Never enough.

Every time I look at that photo it reminds me there was an 'us' before kids. And before us, there was a him and a me. From these humble beginnings, God worked hard to build our family; He designed and planned and helped us walk it out. These four kids completed our family—*thank you, Jesus*—but they are not, and never can be, the center. We are better, stronger, clearer, and more joyful moms when we cling to this truth: *Our family starts and ends with Christ.*

~

Almost thirteen years ago, we stood just outside the bathroom, a pregnancy test laid upside down on the dresser, the soft click of the clock counting the minutes until we could look.

We'd agreed we would both look at the same time. How could one of us know, even a second earlier than the other, if a new chapter was about to begin? How could one little line mean so much? It was as though our entire world was suspended like an overfilled water balloon dangling from the ceiling, and one tiny touch would explode the whole thing.

With a flick of his wrist, Adam flipped it over. An exhale escaped from the recesses of my lungs when my eyes locked onto the unmistakable red plus sign. *I'm going to be a mom.*

Life changed in that moment, as though a lens suddenly slid over my eyes. We both felt the thrill, but also the weight, of that change, and I was thankful when Adam turned to me, smiled, and offered a walk.

We bundled up and took off down the road behind our house, walking in silence at first, the snow crunching beneath our feet. I sucked in the frigid air and let it burn my lungs. My senses seemed amplified, keenly tuned to little details now—the white-washed sky, the stark outline of the trees, the mourning doves and western meadowlarks on the fence posts chirping to each other as if they sensed the news as well.

I glanced at the man next to me, wondering how the same world suddenly looked so different. It was as though somebody had switched out the colors in a crayon box—everything suddenly looked deeper, richer. Blue was no longer just blue; it was indigo or cobalt. I put a curious hand on my stomach, knowing there was nothing to feel yet, but already awash in motherly protection.

My world, our world, shifted that day. It's that simple. The moment your heart locks on to the fact you are a parent, you become a different person. Not better or worse, just different. The assignment has changed. It's like switching prescription glasses with a friend— the blur comes into focus and what was once in focus loses some of its clarity.

We mark that shift with the announcement of a pregnancy. We shower the mom with all the newborn essentials, but by the time the baby is here and the 'new' wears off, she's already in the deep end adjusting to this new perspective, her only choice to sink or swim.

It reminds me of weddings. It's so easy to get caught up in the ceremony or the money spent to create a day we will never forget, that we forsake, or at least relegate to second priority, the support, reminders, care and attention the happy couple will need for the rest of their lives. If I could have spoken to my twenty-something self that day as we walked in the snow, the tender weight of excitement and responsibility pressing down on my shoulders, I would have reminded myself to lean on Adam more and more. I'd have reminded myself that as our family grew, I would not be doing this alone, that it would be okay to need him. It would be good to need him. In fact, it would make me a better mom.

～

Adam likes to challenge me. He gets a nudge, a whisper from the Holy Spirit, and he moves. I love that about him. Okay, I *usually* love that about him. Sometimes it's really annoying.

Like when I came home from a trip one time to find our big-screen TV not only unplugged, but moved into a different room where it was to remain unused for . . . a week? No, a month. Perhaps the entire summer. I was flustered—not at my husband who had seen the filth on TV, worried about what our two-year-old was absorbing, and was similarly concerned about the impact on our own eyes and ears. I loved that he was obedient. I was actually annoyed with *myself*—that I had felt the same, had thought about unplugging the TV, and hadn't.

In our years together, I have yielded more to the idea that this is how a marriage established on Christ is fired and refined. It is fed by the constant striking of two rocks—separate beings with separate convictions carved to fit together, because you don't allow that striking to break you, but to build. And when one rock spins slightly, dips or rolls, the process of redefining your life together begins again.

~

I dropped my oldest off at a morning football camp this summer, and when I came to pick him up, I stood in the bleachers shielding my eyes from the sun to watch the final exercise. The boys faced off two-by-two, and the charge was simple: push, slide, maneuver your opponent as far as you can to the opposite side of the field. Don't tackle or knock them down, just push. One by one, players were eliminated until it came down to two.

An observer next to me mumbled, "Oh it's definitely the guy on the left. He's way bigger. He's going to win." Sure enough, I looked out on the field and caught a glimpse of David and Goliath. The guy on the left had a good foot on the other kid, and when the whistle blew, Goliath muscled him right across the field.

But then it was the coach's turn. The final player, all pads, helmet, and height, faced his coach—a smaller man in a t-shirt and shorts with a look of determination behind the whistle dangling from his mouth. The players formed a circle around the two and watched as their bodies hit. But this time, the coach muscled Goliath all the way to the goal post.

In the final huddle, I listened to the coach reiterate the lesson: it's not about size or strength; it's all about your foundation, your stance, your core. You can spend all your energy wrestling with your arms, your chest or your head, but it really comes down to who has their feet and legs firmly planted.

I can't help but think about our home and the daily, fleshly battles I face as a mother trying to do this journey with joy. I know that Adam is the strength in my core, the steadiness in my stance. Of course, Jesus is always your firm foundation, regardless of who stands beside you, but the people you live with wield incredible influence in your life.

I am grateful Adam is that person next to me. I am grateful he takes note of my independence, my pride, my tendency to build towers where they aren't needed, my impulse to try and do it all. Then, he gently leads me to set down my expectations, my tower building, my insistence that I can do everything—and I choose to follow. That is the signature of a man leading in love. He doesn't make me follow. He doesn't command submission. He loves me in a way that makes me *want* to follow where he's going.

The sooner I lay down my pride and speak truth over us: *I'm not doing this alone, we're in this together, we're on the same team,* I can relax a little bit and discover the joy to be found even in the midst of this incredible, serious assignment of parenthood.

In Dietrich Bonhoeffer's book, *Life Together*, he extols the virtue of experiencing life with another, and reinforces the deep benefit it is to both people: "He who is bearing others knows that he himself is being borne, and only in this strength can he go on bearing." I bear with Adam, and he bears with me, and this alone speaks volumes to our kids about love. I choose, each day, to give him the benefit of the doubt. I assume he has the right heart. I assume he's not going to mess up. I assume that even when he does, he'll do it better next time. There's so much grace. Grace which leads to hope. Hope which leads to joy.

Adam makes me want to be a better mom, a better wife, to pursue Jesus more and more. In college, someone told me to look for the man who would run toward Jesus with me, not always at the same pace or in the same way, but always running.

I'm so glad I listened.

~

There have been some healthy changes for women over the last three decades, and there have been some terrible injustices too. Right now, our world calls women to independence, to focus on the 'me'. *You don't need a husband. You don't need God.* What lies at the heart of that sentiment? Pride. Pure and simple.

In his *Family Letters*, C.S. Lewis once wrote:

> "Pride . . . is the mother of all sin, and the original sin of lucifer . . . an instrument strung, but preferring to play itself because it thinks it knows the tune better than the Musician."

If I am to be more like Christ in my mothering, I have to humble myself. Ironically, when God called me into marriage and parenthood, He was giving me my two greatest lessons in humility. I realized I needed help. I had to come to the place where I could say to Adam, "I don't *have* to do this with you, but I *want* to do this with you, and God wants me to do this with you."

Society is like a river flowing the other way and, I'll be honest, my flesh wants to float right along with it. I want to bear the weight of motherhood without Adam some days, to build my own tower. I hustle, hustle, hustle, and tell myself I'm strong enough, I'm smart enough, I'm capable. Maybe I am, but even if that were so, it would not be in order to glorify myself; it would be to glorify Him.

I don't want to be deceived by the notions of the world, and so I swim upstream knowing Adam is on my team. He is for me. And God is for me too, for our marriage and our family. This isn't to say that you can't experience joy fully if you're a single parent, or your husband has not stepped up to be the spiritual leader of your home. God calls every person to joy, in every season. But it does matter who you yoke yourself to in marriage. It does matter who you share a home with; it undeniably affects every aspect of your life. And it's why I pray, even today, for the future spouses of our kids.

Growing up, my dad always told me relationships are never static, we are always moving closer or further away from one another. I have felt that in my marriage, too. It would be easy to move in the opposite direction from my spouse, not because I want to, or my love for him is diminishing, but because the forces of my flesh and the world would have it that way.

I look at my marriage in the same way I look at my parenting: I don't want to look back on this road and be filled with regret. *How can we have a home where we thrive and not just survive?* I don't want to scratch and claw my way through each day because I couldn't commit to my marriage with joy.

In Philippians 4:4 the apostle Paul exhorts us with these words: "Rejoice in the Lord always. I will say it again: Rejoice!" (NIV). It's a command. Rejoice throughout the day, and watch the transformation take place in your home and in your own heart. And while Paul wrote those words for the community of believers, it's deeply fitting for marriage.

When we become a Christian or get married or have a baby, it would be so convenient to know *then* what lies ahead and if we have the tools in our belt for everything coming our way. Yet God doesn't reveal it all at once—He knows the good parts would overwhelm us, and the bad parts would crush us. We simply couldn't handle knowing everything in advance, and so in this journey of life we experience the wonder and joy that comes with not knowing where it all leads.

That is the magic of wedding vows, yes? I always wondered what would happen if we showed up to a wedding someday and the vows included a list of potential things the couple might face. "Do you promise to stay together when one of you gets cancer, when that house sale falls through, when you go round and round in the same fight, when she miscarries, when you have your first baby and your whole life changes . . .?" You're facing literally a lifetime of unknowns. You commit to a marriage with someone who will be a different person in the future because no one stays the same.

That's why I believe we need Christ at the center—the perfect, sanctifying 'third strand' that keeps us drawn together and ever faithful.

Marriage is also one of the truest models of unconditional love—an earthly archetype of Christ's love for us. In *This Momentary Marriage: A Parable of Permanence*, John Piper writes: "Marriage is not mainly about being or staying in love. It's mainly about telling the truth with our lives. It's about portraying something true about Jesus Christ and the way he relates to his people. It is about showing in real life the glory of the gospel."

Christ keeps us centered when more souls get added to the equation. While many of my strengths were magnified, it seemed all the weaknesses in me when we got married were accentuated and highlighted once we started having kids. And there's a reason for that—any personality shortcoming or propensity to sin will be laid bare in front of your kids at some point. Having kids brings you to the end of yourself because whatever resides in your heart will eventually pour out in your words and actions.

I think of my husband and I walking this journey together, and much like two soldiers or hikers, we are required to bear each other's weight along the way. I cannot be strong at every pass, at every turn. Neither can he. We must, together, go to Christ in our weakness and allow Him to bear the weight of us both.

2 Corinthians 12:9-10 says: "My grace is sufficient for you, for my power is made perfect in weakness. Therefore I will boast all the more gladly of my weaknesses, so that the power of Christ may rest upon me. For the sake of Christ, then, I am content with weaknesses, insults, hardships, persecutions, and calamities. For when I am weak, then I am strong."

I hope our kids will find, in God's perfecting timing, a person who will run toward Jesus with them. I want to share with them the depth of the gift of marriage, but I can't even get my words around it. It's like trying to hold something too big for our hands.

So, when the words won't do it justice, we model it in our actions. We model commitment—sometimes clumsily, sometimes imperfectly, but always faithfully and consistently. And in doing so, our children witness the little strands that continue to weave us together, the friendship, choices, obedience, respect, love. I hope they catch the spontaneous kiss in the car, the way an argument ends without someone leaving. I hope they see that, even after all these years, we still genuinely want to be around each other.

I hope they see that we run toward Christ together, and that together, we model joy.

CHAPTER ELEVEN

SOCKS

Socks. I hate them.

Yet here I was, on a mad dash to find matching socks. I was heading out to meet with a group of highly intelligent, well-read, creative women, and I just knew I would slip off my shoes at the door, shuffle to the living room, and find I was the only one wearing mismatched socks.

So, instead of spending the last five minutes before I left chatting with my husband or pulling one of my kiddos onto my lap, I was distracted by something silly.

Here's the thing: I never, ever manage to have matching socks. Sort them by family member? *Done it.* Buy everyone their own color? *Done it.* Throw them all out and start over? *Done it.* You cannot help me. I will never have matching socks.

That night, it wasn't really about the socks at all. It was about what they represented—the lies I believed about myself and other women.

Every time I showed up someplace with mismatched socks, I was speaking death over myself—I'm disorganized; I don't care about details; I can't plan ahead; I have a messy house; I'm never going to be able to teach my kids how to do things well if I can't do this ONE simple thing.

It's ridiculous, and I'm not doing it anymore. Mama, if you have matching socks on today, I am cheering for you. But I'm guessing it's not socks for you. There's probably something else you feel insecure about, something that says you don't have it all together. Let it go. Period.

I boldly encourage women and mothers around me to find their value and their worth in the One who created them—not their socks or hairstyle or ministry or vehicle, not the likes on their Facebook page or rank in their business, or even number of shoes their kids have. I can't do that if I don't also lead by example.

I desperately want to listen for God's voice in the areas where I need to improve. When He speaks, I want to move. That's obedience, plain and simple. If there are habits in my life that need to be overhauled, I'm in—*if* it's from Him. And when it's not from Him but is coming from a place of condemnation or comparison, I'm letting it go. When it's coming from self-imposed vanity, I'm letting it go. When it's based on the standards of this world, I'm letting it go. When it's a function of tower-building, I'm letting it go.

I'm not trying to get out of doing the work; I'm trying to make sure my energy is spent on the *right* things. And right now, it's not matching socks. Guess what? I sat down at that meeting and I couldn't tell you who had matching socks. I was too busy listening to the wisdom, the laughter, the ideas, the other mamas on fire for Jesus who wanted to choose the best education for their kids and serve their community well. I was too busy asking questions and leaning in for answers. I was too busy with the more important things.

~

Scripture tells us to be fervent and focused, alive in the things of God, not of the world. Romans 12:11-12 is clear: "Do not be slothful in zeal, be fervent in spirit, serve the Lord. Rejoice in hope, be patient in tribulation, be constant in prayer."

There are six clear commands in these verses: do not be slothful, be fervent, rejoice in hope, serve, be patient, and pray consistently.

Really, is there a verse better suited for motherhood? Do not fall asleep, mothers! Be fervent in spirit, and if you are losing your energy to stay fervent, perhaps it's time to reflect on where your energy is going.

Far too much of my energy has gone into 'stuff'. You know what I'm talking about—the slow overwhelm of your home with *all the things*. My husband has spent many years patiently working around the piles I have made in our house, gently persuading me to downsize, organize, and simplify. I tried—sort of—until God took a different approach.

I asked a friend to evaluate some areas of my life. "Give it to me straight," I told her. The strengths she highlighted affirmed and encouraged me, but one specific word she gave me struck my soul. She said I can be "scattered." *Ouch.*

Hands full? Sure. Emotional at times? That's okay. But scattered? No. I don't want to be scattered. I want to be steady, reliable, focused. And I have noticed something during the past decade: when I am surrounded by more things, I'm scattered. I'm distracted. I'm weighed down.

Proverbs 14:1 says, "The wisest of women builds her house, but folly with her own hands tears it down." My house needs to be built not with more material possessions, but with things of eternal value. I want to be more worried about my children's spiritual integrity than I am about the latest home gadgets.

I'm not an out-of-control spender, but I have more material possessions than I could ever need or want. Matthew 6:19-21 says, "Do not lay up for yourselves treasures on earth, where moth and rust destroy and where thieves break in and steal, but lay up for yourselves treasures in heaven, where neither moth nor rust destroys and where thieves do not break in and steal. For where your treasure is, there your heart will be also."

This isn't an anti-prosperity message but a get-your-priorities-straight message. And it should be a battle cry for mamas everywhere.

Having money is not a sin. Buying things is not a sin. But chasing after material possessions is one of the fastest ways to hinder your growth, keep you in a cycle of discontent, and steal your peace. Whether you're trying to create a beautiful home, create a comfortable life, or satisfy your kids, this pursuit will keep you from living an on-fire, joy-filled journey. It will make you a distracted mom.

Proverbs 31 paints a vibrant picture of a rock-star mom and wife. Dang, does anybody else get a little intimidated by her? This girl was not messing around. She had it together, and dare I say, she might have even had matching socks. And sewed them herself.

But here's the thing: I don't think God gave us the description of this woman to make us feel like we can never live up to her standards. Instead, He painted a picture of how to set our priorities. What I really see in her example is her heart. "A wife of noble character who can find? . . . She watches over the affairs of her household and does not eat the bread of idleness" (Proverbs 31:10, 27 NIV).

This woman is a master curator of her time and possessions. The definition of idleness is not just sitting around doing nothing. Idleness is doing life passively, to be lethargic, slothful, stopping short of whatever propels us forward. It's getting in the driver's seat of the car but just spinning the tires.

Along with my schedule, God's message to me has been clear: prune the stuff. Quit running around simply managing it, because it's getting in the way—literally and figuratively—of what I want you to be engaging with.

You own it, and it owns you. Why? Because it owns your time; it owns your head space. It doesn't matter what your income is, you can still be distracted by the Dollar Store or Macy's. Whether your house is a mansion or an apartment, whether you have overflowing bank accounts or are just scraping by, it's time to seriously ask yourself what has a hold on you and what consumes your time and attention.

The way you navigate the constant onslaught from society telling us that more is better and bigger will impact your children forever. You don't need all the things, and they don't need all the things— not when they were babies, not when they're in middle school, and not when they're grown.

God has gotten a hold of my heart on this because it affects the way I walk out my faith, the way I mother, and the way I build our home with Adam. My kids need Jesus; they need my time; they need to make memories. We utilize money and resources as a bridge to get there sometimes. And other times we look down and realize we're building another tower. That's when it's time to let some of it go and ask the Holy Spirit for another way to get there. And trust me, He always provides another way.

Command those who are rich in this present world not to be arrogant nor to put their hope in wealth, which is so uncertain, but to put their hope in God, who richly provides us with everything for our enjoyment.

1 Timothy 6:17 NIV

~

It was the dead of night when my friend's house started to burn. No alarms sounded. Sleeping beside her husband, she woke to the crackling of flames. All five of their children slept downstairs. They all made it out alive thanks to their quick thinking, a passing deputy who ran in and grabbed one of their kiddos, and the grace of God. But that night, they had to watch as their beautiful home burned to the ground.

The sun came up, and while the rest of us were tackling our morning routines, they were coming to grips with the fact that nearly every material possession they had on this earth had been lost. When I heard the news from a mutual friend at church, I backed up against the wall, the shock overwhelming, my words catching in a lump in my throat.

They were all alive, *thank you, Jesus*. But all of their stuff was gone. All of it—her purse, their favorite books highlighted and underlined, that sweater from college, the stuffed walrus from the zoo that their kid sleeps with every night, earrings from their wedding, all the photo albums . . .

Think of all the things we accumulate over time, the precious mementos we take from key moments in our lives, the things passed down. My friend's husband built their kids' beds using his grandfather's tools. It was all gone. They can't get it back. Ever.

And yet, there was joy there. As God would have it, this is the very friend who has gone a long way in teaching me, through grace and love and many noisy playdates, that less is more. Every item in her home has a purpose. She doesn't keep extra clothes. There are no bulging drawers, closets, or hampers. She has mastered the idea that it's okay to have extra space in a room, that it's good and healthy to have buffers in your home and in your life. Not every single space has to overlap seam to seam. She maintains a minimalistic prowess cultivated by years of practice and discipline. She has been careful, specific, purposeful.

When their house burned down, she grieved, but she maintained that same eternal perspective she cultivated in the years leading up to the fire. The first time I spoke with her afterward, she said, "Yes, this is so hard. But our babies are here. And we're here. And stuff is only stuff."

When we became first-time parents, I accepted, purchased, and allowed a free flow of all the things into our home—extra bags of clothes from friends, toys and souvenirs at every outing, more silverware in my kitchen drawer than we would ever need. Now I realize we just don't need all the things.

When we had infants, my arms, head, and heart were so full I could hardly think straight. Too much stuff was part of the reason I was so exhausted. I don't need to be a minimalist; I just need to pay attention to how more and more stuff detracts me from joy. And I'm getting there. If it's holding a place in our home, if it's getting a slice of our bank account, we count the cost.

Just how many times will I pick up that little one-dollar toy before I walk over to the garbage can, toss it in, and choose to spend those extra five minutes in the Word, on the floor with my toddler, in conversation with Adam, or doing something that nurtures my soul and might potentially move the needle toward our goals? I'm now in a season, a life-giving season, of not only clearing my schedule more, but letting physical things go. Whether it's to the garbage, to a local organization, or to family and friends, it's gone from my house. My stuff cannot have a hold on me anymore.

With God's help, I'm clearing my house and my mind, and I'm setting a steadfast example for my kiddos on where our real treasure is. I understand that nothing I hold in my hands will go with me when I stand before God. But the truth is, deep down I'm a hopeless sentimental. And if I'm totally honest, even in a season of pruning there are things I just don't want to let go.

I'm thinking of the glass bottle, as big as my index finger, that carries two drops of my grandmother's perfume. I open that lid, and if I close my eyes I am in their home in Riverton, Wyoming— my lips against a metal can of orange juice, Grandma ironing Grandpa's snap-button dress shirts, raspberry vines crawling across the back garden.

When my best friend got married, she wrapped her bridesmaids' presents in sheer pink ribbon. I kept that ribbon, wrapped it around the stick shift in my car, and it stayed there for eight years. When we took Brooke for her one-year pictures, I pulled it from the car and wrapped it around her ponytail.

Last night I slipped a ratty night gown over my head. It's white with red and black xoxo's stamped all over it. My mom, who dropped it off at my dorm room in a Valentine's Day basket during college, has since gifted me other pajamas, soft and comfortable, but I still slip on that Valentine's night gown.

There's more and more: the note Leslee left on the windshield of my car on the last day of my job as a reporter, reminding me to celebrate this new chapter unfolding; Tarrin's sixteenth birthday gift: an over-sized Mason jar, modge-podged with magazine cutouts from our favorite boy bands and inside high school jokes; Alison's clay frog, hand-molded in art class; my little sister's first dance shoes.

I love it all. Deep down, I'm holding on to these items because, really, I'm holding on to people. I'm clinging to the memories, the relationships. There's nothing wrong with keeping a few mementos, but I'm hearing God more clearly on this: hold on to the people, and let the stuff go. I want less of the things that don't matter because it opens a whole world of freedom. It frees up time, it frees up head space, and most importantly, it frees up my heart.

I want more of these people, more photographs, more time, more memories. And if the people are gone, I can honor them by living a life worthy of my calling—a life not weighed down by stuff or by the pursuit of more things, but a life lived with intention and joy.

I imagine myself standing before Jesus with that bottle of perfume tucked in my pocket, a few dusty boxes at my feet containing Elijah's first onesie folded with care, Hannah's first smudged painting with the yellow sun, a journal of love notes and dried pressed flowers Adam and I mailed back and forth to each other when we dated long distance.

"Just leave them there," He whispers. "Just leave them and come with me."

CHAPTER TWELVE

MOMS EVERYWHERE

The first year we were married we packed everything we owned, crammed it into a storage unit, and flew to a small town in Ethiopia for two months to minister to refugee children.

In those first couple of days we experienced an overwhelming cacophony of new colors, smells, and tastes. My stomach struggled to adjust to the roadside mangoes, the spongy, sour bread we dipped into soup, and the traditional shot of thick black coffee in the afternoon. We shopped at the market, circling around waist-high sacks of pepper, garlic, and sugar. Two miles out of town, hyenas clawed at the filth and children searched for food scraps at the garbage dump. Further along the road kids kicked a ball past ancient, ornate churches, and limes and potatoes were laid out for sale on blankets at the street corners.

The vibrancy and beauty were undeniable. The red clay at our feet took on an orangish hue in the morning sunrise, dark-skinned women wrapped themselves in scarves of every color, and the thick, ancient walls reminded me of another time and place in history. But my mind struggled to reconcile such unfiltered beauty with the immense poverty all around us. We slept on the floor, and cockroaches scattered when I opened the cabinets. There was no air conditioning, no running water, refrigerator or kitchen appliances, no working toilets.

On laundry days, I gathered with the women around piles of dirty clothes. Pouring jugs of water and sprinkling powdered soap into metal bins, we submerged each piece one by one. We worked like that for hours, hunched in a circle on the hard ground, scrubbing each piece of clothing by hand.

My legs were numb, my fingers were swollen and wrinkled like grapes, and my back was aching. But I quickly realized I was witnessing the fabric of friendship and community being woven before my eyes. Chores took longer there, and meals were prepared from scratch, but the women worked together with a steady determination. Their conversation was the same—unhurried and intentional.

One morning I woke at sunrise to wander the countryside before the market came alive with life and work. For the first time in my life, my skin color cast me into the minority. I had not seen another Caucasian for weeks. A few days earlier, a curious girl on the road had stared at me. She told our friends we were the first white people she had ever seen. She asked to see my arm, running her fingers over my freckles, marveling at my skin, concerned the white color meant I had a disease.

The street children swarmed around us. Hundreds more lined the streets, begging, all day. One girl sat in the sun, breastfeeding an infant. Her house was a three by four-foot tent made of branches, scrap plastic, and old blankets. I didn't know what she slept on or where she went to the bathroom. Her younger sister memorized my route and trailed at my side with grimy hands, clinging, pleading for whatever money I might have in my pocket, reaching for the bunch of bananas I had tucked under my arm. Her hair was woven against her head in tight, greasy curls. Her feet were bare. She latched on to my arms, pulling me down so she could kiss my arms and cheeks, mango bits and juice dribbling down her chin smearing onto my forearms and shirt.

One day she grabbed me around the waist in a tight hug and motioned to her mouth that she wanted food. Before I knew what was happening, she had cupped her hands around one of my breasts and was about to put her mouth on it before I stopped her. Flustered, I gave her the food in my arms and a small hug, then caught up with Adam. I still think about that girl to this day. *Where is she now? Did she survive? Does she have her own babies now? Are they hungry? What hopes and dreams does she have for them?*

Our time in Africa widened the lens of my camera and allowed me to see there are mothers all over the earth, all wanting the same thing but with incredibly different resources. The mothers I met there faced entirely different battles than what I face in America, but our goal is still the same: obedience, relationship, joy. Not just surviving, not performing, but truly becoming who He made us to be through a transformation of our hearts.

We are all on different continents, but we will not grow weary in doing good. We will not grow weary, because we have His joy.

~

The moment the wheels of the plane left the runway, we said we would go back. I still think of the women there; I check plane ticket prices and look at the calendar. The Ethiopian family we stayed with remain friends and they emphatically say, "Yes, please come, and bring all four."

What a reunion that will be. I am no longer that naïve, energetic, career-driven twenty-something from so many years ago, fresh into marriage, not ready for kids. "Here I am," I'd say, wrapping them in a bear hug, "I'm a mom now, four times over."

Someday, we will take our kids there. I want them to see, as I did, how different our lives are, yet in deeper ways, we are all the same. And I want to go back as a mother, because I know I would see the place, our friends, the moms, differently. How could I not?

What does this experience have to teach me in this current season? We must not grow weary, no matter our circumstance or situation. The women I met in Ethiopia illustrated that through their deep friendships, their kindness to one another, their consistency with their children, and their labor of love for their homes, land, husbands, and families. In them, I saw a kind of steely determination not to trade even a sliver of joy for something lesser.

I think of the hundreds of daily tasks that separate our lives from theirs. The danger for us is not so much about physical survival; more likely it is a spiritual apathy caused by our relative prosperity. The landscape of their life is so different from mine, but those women in Ethiopia are drawing from the same well—Christ.

Joy is never situational. The mothers in Africa are called to the same holiness as I am. They, too, are called to live with joy, to rebuke fear, to keep the first things first.

There's something beautiful about the tapestry of God's design—moms on every continent, experiencing joy in the deepest recesses of their soul despite circumstances or social status. The hard truth is that no matter our life situation, no one will do this for us—not in Africa, not in Italy, not in Wyoming, not wherever you live. *You* have to make the decision. *You* have to pursue Christ and choose joy.

We all need to be reconciled to something bigger than ourselves. It is too easy to be defined by our circumstances, our location, our background. I believe God calls all mothers from all walks of life to abundant, life-giving joy.

∼

The night before we left Ethiopia, shadows danced across the walls as we played cards by candlelight. Outside, an evening storm pummeled the clay earth.

I stared at their dark faces, the laugh lines that played at the edges of their eyes as if chasing something. Suddenly I wished I could stay a little longer—long enough to etch their faces into my memory. I wanted to capture this feeling, this realization that it took me flying to the other side of the world to forget about myself for a little while and concentrate on someone else's needs.

The following morning we said goodbye, tears falling on the muddy ground as we jumped puddles and hauled our luggage to a waiting van. One little girl wrapped her arms around my waist, and I mumbled our favorite phrase to overcome the lump in my throat, "We will meet again, *inshallah.*" If God wills it.

~

Two days later, I attended my first major league baseball game at Comerica Park in downtown Detroit. It had felt fabulous to climb into a real bed, feel the hot water pour over my body in the shower, and order a pizza, but I was overwhelmed by the luxuries—cell phones and sidewalks, not one home but two, perhaps even a house on wheels to haul to a campground, manicured lawns and hands and feet, and money, money, money.

Dizzy with heat and culture shock, the towering skyscrapers, salaries of the men playing the game on the field, the exorbitant price of a cup of lemonade, all seemed so excessive.

Suddenly, I missed Africa. I could see the women washing their hair—heads bent over a steel pan, cold water and shampoo dripping from coarse black tendrils. I could hear the pinched howls of hyenas searching the streets for stray cats and dogs at night; I could see the acacia trees silhouetted against the skyline.

Meeting women, children and babies from another country laid a foundation in my motherhood long before I became a mother. I lament the poverty and the wars that have torn at the fabric of communities and altered family legacies with death and disease and corruption. But I do not pity those mothers, and they do not pity me. The mother I stay in contact with aches for the same things I ache for—more of God, safety for her babies, and a home filled with joy.

My time in Africa helped prepare me for motherhood in a profound way, encouraging me to keep an eternal perspective when it's all too easy to get distracted with material wealth. I am reminded to stay tethered to God's heart, to return to relationship, to not get too comfortable with all the *things*. No matter where I live, or how much or little I have, it's always about my heart. Raising these kiddos is always about the heart.

I think of our time in Ethiopia, and I'm reminded of the lessons learned in this experience of cross-cultural motherhood. That is why I'm desiring less and less stuff and instead pursuing more— more people, more experiences, more memories, more eternal value-chasing. More heart.

CHAPTER THIRTEEN

SURRENDER

Last night, Adam took three of our four kids to the lake to do some night fishing. Yes, I said 'night fishing'. Not just going to the lake for the afternoon, but fishing on the boat in pitch darkness, using a bow and arrow to spear carp with shiny gold scales as big as your thumb. There's no place like the lake at midnight. The water stretches out like glass. It's stunningly serene, every noise clear and amplified by the silence—the plop of a fish, the hum of a mosquito, the call of the loons.

At dusk, I kissed them goodbye and ran my fingers along the side of the boat as it lurched forward on the trailer. I stayed in our dusty garage in the lingering silence for a few minutes and let my mind wander to the what ifs, a mine of dark places that would be easy enough to get lost in.

Unspeakable things can happen to your children, to the people you love most in this world. It's why I truly believe God designed parenthood to draw us out into the deep and learn to fully surrender.

Water has never been my thing. Wyoming is about as far from the ocean as you can get, and I only have a handful of memories of being at the lake growing up. I swam at the local pool, but life at the lake has always felt a bit foreign to me.

As God would have it, I married a man who grew up in Michigan and my in-laws now spend part of their year in Florida, so I've grown to love the water—the beach, the waves, the lakes. And yet there's still a sliver of my soul that feels uneasy every time we are out on the water. Brooke almost drowning in the bathtub left its mark on my soul. Water continues to be a tangible reminder to me of our vulnerability, that I'm not fully in control.

By the age of two, Elijah was already a natural fisherman. With rod in hand and a steeled look of determination across his face, he'd head off with his dad. That's when I realized that being on the water would be part of our life, and the fear I held on to from the tub incident would have to be wholly surrendered.

We have witnessed Elijah's love of the outdoors unfold over the last decade, giving him a resilience borne through long hours of learning. His feet are like bear pads now, callused and coarse from the rocks, the sand, the hikes. He has mastered 'the catch', most of them by hand—turtles, lizards, fish, rabbits, squirrels. He catches snakes, no matter the species, no matter the size—milk snakes, garter snakes, bull snakes, rattle snakes—fascinated by their markings and predatory tactics.

When Elijah is fishing it's like a light has flipped on inside him. He's firing on all cylinders, like a bird taking flight, its wings spreading, flying. And as his mama who wants to help him pursue this passion, I can't clip his wings because of my fear. Instead, I create a few boundaries and release him—to run, fish, dream, adventure, chase, catch, collect, learn.

A friend told me she couldn't let her son and husband go ice fishing because she harbors the same kind of fears I have—fears of that thick, sturdy ice giving way beneath their feet, and the people she loves most slipping into the icy water. And I agreed with her; I was scared, too.

But this is the trap of fear. It lets you think that if you somehow avoid the situation, you will avoid the pain, the potential risk, the "I told you so" if something happens. That's not true. If something bad happens, it doesn't matter if you feared it or not. A decade ago, I was still holding onto that notion though. So, when they first started fishing, I overcompensated. I thought if I voiced my concerns, I could lean on that if something happened. I nagged; I grumbled; I complained. "Do they have life jackets on? How could you stay so late? How thick was the ice? No really, how thick?"

That isn't trust. That isn't surrender to Christ. That isn't even a semblance of giving it all to God. Instead, it is me willfully hovering over something I told Him I had given Him years ago. So, I had a decision to make: to release it all—or not.

I'm not just fearful about losing them physically; it's the idea of them leaving this earth before I do that scares me. There's also fear in relation to their minds and souls. My greatest fear is our kids dying, whether now or when they're older, having rejected their

Savior. I want them to walk in the fullness of all He has designed them to be and experience here on earth, but even more than that, I want them to rest in eternity with Him.

It seems so simple, but God tells us not to fear, and when we do, to cast it all on Him. I like to picture all the ways I can transfer my anxious thoughts onto Him—laying them at His feet, throwing them, giving them up, handing them over, releasing them.

Fear may not change the outcome, but it does wreck my mind, weaken my trust in God, and keep me preoccupied instead of focused on Him. Standing in the garage that night, my mind racing with all the possibilities of what could happen out on the lake, or on the drive there or the drive back—it was sucking the joy out of my heart.

Fear is an emotion; it's legitimate and real, but it's only one of many feelings God gifted us with when He created our mortal bodies and minds. It was never supposed to control us, to steer the ship. 1 John 4:18 says, "There is no fear in love, but perfect love casts out fear. For fear has to do with punishment, and whoever fears has not been perfected in love."

Moms, you could sit in fear all day, literally every moment, contemplating all the ways life could render tragedy at any turn, reflecting on the moment-by-moment realities of your children living in a fallen world. And if you allowed that fear to take over, you could be completely consumed.

Fear is mentioned more than five hundred times in the Bible, but the phrase "fear not" is said 365 times—a perfect fit for every day of the calendar year. God knew, oh how He knew, that fear would captivate our hearts, make us toil, and enslave us.

Perhaps no fear has so much potential to paralyze us as the 'fear of man'. I still worry plenty about what other people think about my mothering. *Are we making the right decisions about schooling, holding off on cell phones, sleepovers, sugar, school sports, our expectations for grades, bedtime, what they wear, what age to start a checking account, what friends they cleave to, what books they read, how to discipline, how to talk to them about sex and marriage and friendship and life consequences?*

I worry that someday my kids will wake up and all the ways I failed will slowly start to pop up in their lives in the form of bad habits, that whatever wounds or hurts they experienced during their childhood will change the course of their life. This fear can be paralyzing, overwhelming. But the older I get, the more I am dismantling that tower of fear. The fact is, I will never get this all right, and that's okay. He tells me to "fear not." Thank you, Jesus.

If I am still fearful of not doing motherhood well, it's not because of what others think or how they will judge, but because I don't want to squander something so precious that God has gifted me. This is the kind of fear that takes my breath away.

God is molding my heart on this, still, because it is easily a place of bondage for me, a place where my spirit of joy is stolen. I have to make a choice daily, sometimes hourly, to rest in this simple verse in Luke 18:16: "But Jesus called them to him, saying, 'Let the children come to me, and do not hinder them, for to such belongs the kingdom of God.'"

If I think that *I* am responsible for shaping my children's hearts, I'm giving myself too much credit. I'm here to love them and lead them to Christ, but I cannot save them. That's the work of the Holy Spirit.

If I operate in a spirit of fear, I squelch the opportunities, so numerous every day, for my kids to experience His peace. The trials and tribulations they must experience as they grow are not meant to hinder or disable them but transform them. Their own journey will be their own journey, and I need not fear it. Instead, I pray that in each of their future relationships—their spouses, friendships, the people in their workplaces and in their community—their wounds would be healed, their minds would be full of wisdom from every experience, good and bad, and their attitudes and spirits would be overflowing with Christ's joy.

I do not have room for fear. I must willfully, purposefully, cast my anxiety onto Him, lay my fears at His feet, and ask Him for deliverance from the bondage of fear. I invite you to do the same, to not just cast out fear but chase it away. Can we boldly proclaim this over our homes, our marriages, and our children? *Fear, you're not welcome here—not in my head, not in my home. You're not welcome to suck the life and joy out of this journey.*

~

I stood in that dusty garage and I set my mind on this: I have a husband who so desires time with his kids that he packs the food, the life jackets, the sunscreen, and the blankets, and he takes them to his favorite place to make memories.

I set my mind on this: my kids will return tomorrow, their hands stinky with the smell of trout and carp, their shoulders pink from the sun, their eyes watery and wild from a day of adventure.

I set my mind on this: we will have fresh walleye for dinner tomorrow night; my husband will slide into the sheets next to me, and he'll be there when I wake up.

And I set my mind on this: I am deeply grateful for all of it. I will trust God, and I will choose to be a mama who says goodbye when they pull out of the garage with genuine joy—for really, they are off to spread their wings and fly.

CHAPTER FOURTEEN

GO BACK

The nursing home smells like linoleum and Band-Aids. My mom takes my hand and gently leads me down hallways of thin, worn carpet. A nurse wipes biscuits and gravy from the dinner tables, and a back-door alarm sounds—a steady, monotone beep that rings in my ears. A woman mumbles as she rolls up and down the hallway in her wheelchair using her heels to pull herself along like a snail. Most of the residents rest in their rooms for the evening, a blanket placed over their laps, waiting. So much waiting.

In a tandem effort with the night nurses, we walk from room to room inviting and wheeling residents out to the foyer where we gather in a circle. And then we read—nothing of significance, nothing of persuasion. Just short inspirational stories to help them laugh and think.

~

What I remember most about those nights is my mom. In her, I witnessed tenderness at work. I saw her love on people. She held their hands, caressed paper-thin skin, carried cups of ice water, dabbed Kleenex at watery eyes, leaned in to ask about the hip pain or adjust an afghan.

If I'm honest, I didn't really want to be there at first. The oxygen tanks, pills and heart monitors made me uneasy. In my youth, it seemed a lot like watching flames grow dimmer, lives that had once been full and on fire now just a flicker, the waxing of energy.

But they always loved it when my mom brought me with her, as if my youthfulness triggered memories of their own kids and grandkids. They slipped butterscotch candies into my hands and told me stories, reliving a highlight reel that seemed to keep them afloat and give them hope. Eventually I learned their names, remembered the repeated stories, and looked forward to those trips to the nursing home.

I thought about them long after we left, and my heart ached a little. We forget the elderly lived a life before us. Were they not once the decision-makers, the movers, the up-and-comers, the new generation? Were they not once *us*? And how many of them were mothers? What simple, profound lessons had been carved from their stories and experiences?

My mom understood that in a way I couldn't grasp then. Looking back, I can see this was one of the places where she shined. And this will be part of her legacy—pure, unadulterated kindness.

It makes me wonder: *What legacy am I shaping for our four kids? What am I teaching them even when I don't realize they are watching, listening?* I know without a doubt that one of the places I want them to follow me, to step securely into my footsteps, is into a community of believers—to engage fully and be vulnerable, consistent, serving, leading wherever they are called.

I want my kids to go to church.

~

I drove back to Wyoming a few months ago. Walking from my mom's house to my dad's office for lunch, I marveled at the dozens of crab apple trees that had bloomed that week, dressing the streets in white and pink petals. The colors always seem deeper and sharper in the spring, as if God just dipped the world in water and it has all come up clean.

I never thought I could come back here to live and raise a family because a new life would tromp all over my carefully curated memories, like paving a shiny new road over an old country lane. When I do come back, I visit all the places that have a piece of my heart and sit a while, allowing myself to feel gratefulness, remorse, hope. What if we did that more often with our past?

They say that grounding—the process of walking barefoot on the earth, feeling the dirt and dust, grass, and rocks—is healthy for your mind and body. I think about the visceral experience of walking where you used to walk, to remember where you have been and to touch those places in a tangible way. What if you returned to the halls of the elementary school, lay down on the bunk bed in that first dorm room, sat on the side of the road at the mile marker where you wrecked your car in college?

Whether it might heal wounds, stir up emotions that have long been numbed, or bring you deep contentment, there's something significant about going back. I like meeting the parents of friends I didn't know growing up, getting a glimpse of the people who shaped them. It's incredibly revealing. The people and experiences from your past don't define you any more than the present, but they do have the ability to reveal insights we couldn't have gathered any other way.

Part of why I am the way I am is because of where and who I come from. I feel I have lived lifetimes in my hometown—my childhood split into two chapters by my parents' divorce, then a new chapter beginning after I moved out to attend the local community college.

When I visit my childhood home, I crisscross town from the first newspaper I interned at on Main Street, to Alison's country home, Southside Elementary School, my old dorm room, the streets bordering Tarrin's house where we walked for hours, the home my parents built together when I was a toddler, and the drive-in movie theater where I earned my first paychecks cleaning up popcorn buckets, condom wrappers and the occasional dollar bill off the dirt ground.

And then my church. I always go to the church.

Maybe it was the brightness of spring, or a recent cancer diagnosis in our family, but on this particular trip, a wave of nostalgia rolled over me when I drove past. I had to stop. I have spent countless hours in this church—two decades of Sunday School and sermons, potlucks, baptisms, weddings, and so many conversations. I know every inch of the building, the best hiding spots (up in the balcony behind the last row of pews), where they keep cookies in the kitchen, the layout of the pastor's office, which doors creak, how the plush red carpet feels beneath my feet in the fellowship hall, the sound of the organ in the chapel.

In middle school, the pastor's wife invited a friend and me to re-catalogue the library adjacent to the sanctuary. We sat on the floor in the evenings, sipped on ginger ale, and indexed every book.

On Palm Sunday, we waved oversized palm leaves to remember Jesus' arrival into Jerusalem, and I sat next to my parents the remainder of service, twisting the waxy leaves around my little fingers and folding them into rings and crosses.

Every Christmas Eve was spent there. We each held a lit candle; the final song was an acapella version of 'Silent Night'. As a child it took my breath away—our faces illuminated by the flicker of flames, our voices melding together like the wax at my fingertips, the world's problems suspended for just a few minutes.

I was married beneath the cross at the front altar under the focal point of the vaulted ceilings, surrounded by the blues, reds and oranges of the stained glass in the sanctuary.

I am so grateful this church was a part of the foundation of my faith. I know this isn't what church looked like or felt like for everyone growing up, and it took me years to understand that. I know there are people who tie their early church experience to their pain in the same way I tie it to the birth of my faith. I know there is abuse, politicking, mismanagement, and loneliness. I know the Holy Spirit isn't welcome in some spaces, and people argue about the music, the lights, the seating, whether the pastor should wear a suit or jeans. The reality is, we're gathering a bunch of sinners, people at all different points along the way, with varying theologies, life experience and social status—you bet there's going to be some pain and disagreement.

Yet, there's also space for breakthrough, forgiveness, revelation, maturity, friendship, and a casting out of the dark so we can be led by the light and go back out into the world a little steadier, a little more loved.

Church engagement is not a salvation issue. Baptism isn't going to save your soul. Communion isn't going to save your soul. Going to a church isn't going to save your soul. Jesus already did that work for you on the cross. But each of those steps goes a long way in building the foundation of your faith.

C.S. Lewis noticed something about himself when he became a Christian—he didn't want to go to church. Can you imagine? One of the greatest theologians in history wanted to study, pray, and worship in the privacy of his home.

Then he had a change of heart. In *God in the Dock* he wrote,

> "I disliked very much their hymns, which I considered to be fifth-rate poems set to sixth-rate music. But as I went on, I saw the great merit of it. I came up against different people of quite different outlooks and different education, and then gradually my conceit just began peeling off. I realized that the hymns (which were just sixth-rate music) were, nevertheless, being

sung with devotion and benefit by an old saint in elastic-side boots in the opposite pew, and then you realize that you aren't fit to clean those boots. It gets you out of your solitary conceit."

Solitary conceit. Ouch. Thank you, Mr. Lewis, there is no better term for it. If there's ever a reason for me not to want to go to church, it's usually about me. Me, me, me.

Yet what if God wants me at church today for reasons that have nothing to do with me, like helping other mothers walk in obedience to Christ? Am I so wrapped up in trying to be good at this mothering thing that I miss out on what God wants to do *through* me?

1 Peter 2:16 tells us not to use our freedom as a "cloak for vice." I believe this applies to church, too. You have the freedom to skip it—but don't. In a community of believers, it's okay to be surrounded by people unlike you. In fact, that's the point. It's okay if you're shy, unsteady, unkempt, unsure, extroverted or introverted—all of us are called to church fellowship. Communion with believers (and nonbelievers who come to church) trumps personalities, for as C.S. Lewis wrote in his *Collected Letters:*

> "The Church is not a human society of people united by their natural affinities, but the Body of Christ, in which all members, however different (and He rejoices in their differences and by no means wishes to iron them out) must share the common life, complementing and helping one another precisely by their differences."

Paul expresses the same conviction in 1 Corinthians 12:12-14 with these words: "Just as a body, though one, has many parts, but all its many parts form one body, so it is with Christ. For we were all baptized by one Spirit so as to form one body . . . Even so the body is not made up of one part but of many" (NIV).

We are now members of a church that looks nothing like that church I grew up in—not tangibly anyway. There are no stained-glass windows or church choir swaying in blue robes; there is no benediction, no nervous kids traversing to the front of the church, their shaky hands clutching an acolyte candle. Instead, we sit on comfy chairs and watch a well-edited video of announcements on a big screen. I keep my Bible splayed open on my lap, flipping to the verses to follow along even as they are illuminated in front of me.

I used to let little things distract me—our pastor taking too many rabbit trails, the music being too loud—but when my mind goes there, I realize I'm headed off-track; I'm on a road to making this church a religion and not a relationship.

Instead I want to approach each gathering with joy, with the expectation that I'm coming to meet God, to gently and purposefully lay aside my wandering eyes, the weight of the week, the hundreds of text messages and emails and conversations and plans—and to hear from Him. I thank Him, over and over, that I get to be here. I don't come to be entertained or strung along or dazzled. I don't need every element of the service to be perfect. If I'd like to see something changed, I go through the proper channels, or I take the time to serve on whatever team is in charge of that particular area. Until then, I get my head and heart in a mind of worship, and I just come.

In *Mere Christianity,* Lewis wrote: "If you want to get warm you must stand near the fire: if you want to be wet you must get into the water. If you want joy, power, peace, eternal life, you must get close to, or even into, the thing that has them."

Church is not the fire, but it is the gathering of people pursuing the fire. Whatever faith you come into motherhood with, the questions remain: What do you want for your kids that is eternity-centric? What steps will they trace when you're gone? What ground will they go back and cover? And will it include authentic, genuine engagement and worship with a local body of believers?

God loves when we willingly gather with people we might not have otherwise met or spent any time with. I look around my church, and it thrills me to see the young and old, the mismatched and the messy, the have-it-all-togethers. We all walk in carrying something. The young man who contemplated suicide last week might sit near the proud grandpa who just attended his granddaughter's high school graduation, and he is sitting near the couple who had a fight on the way here. It can feel like baggage, the weight of the world ushered into the sanctuary with us. But it's a swirl of stories, and God cares about it all.

When we are the Church and we are doing it right, we fling open the doors, invite the believers and the unbelievers alike, and we come together. We don't compromise His Word or strip the Gospel of its power or get distracted. We pray, worship, teach the truth, and follow Jesus. And just like in friendship or in marriage, we come back again and again, even when we disagree, even when it hurts. That is how our spiritual muscle is built. That is when the world watches—to see if we disintegrate, to see if we walk away.

And that's the essence of the Gospel, isn't it? Are we willing to love others, to find the lovely in the unlovely? Do we do the uncomfortable thing and sit by the new person? Do we talk to them, get to know them? Or do we get so busy, so inwardly focused on our tight circle of friends, that we fail to see with the eyes of Jesus? I don't want to just play Church—I want to *be* the Church. I want to do the hard things because Jesus did the hard things. He did the hard things because He shared the heart of the Father.

In the book of Jonah, God directed him to Nineveh to tell the people the truth: They were headed in the wrong direction, and they needed to repent. Yet, he wouldn't do it. He ran, and we know where he ended up—hanging out in the stomach cavity of a sea monster. Why was his heart so set against God's command? Because he wasn't broken for them. He lacked compassion for the lost.

How can we help people, serve friends, tell them the truth if we aren't broken for them, aching for them, our hearts wanting the very best for them? We can't. It's that simple.

It reminds me of the story of the prodigal son. It dawned on me several years ago that I was never the prodigal. I have always been the older brother who stayed home—the one who stayed and worked, keyed in on the moves of my parents, focused desperately on pleasing them and doing the right things. And then when the prodigal returned—much to everyone's delight—I was the sibling sulking in the background. *Well, how come I stuck around and did the right thing if they got to go out and play?* I was puffed up with pride, not filled with sorrow or concern for the lost sheep. My heart was as much in the wrong place as the prodigal's. I had to do some serious repenting.

If we modeled our church after Jesus, can you imagine the transformations that might take place? He did life with others so well and so honestly. Jesus had His circle, and He loved them perfectly and hard. But He spent equal energy seeking, finding, and inviting those who needed hope—the ones who were unloved, lost, sick, and thought they had it all together—and He wooed them to the one thing that could heal them, complete them, and bring them lasting joy.

In contrast, the Pharisees were religious people who followed the law to a tee, even tithing on the spices they purchased in the market! But they had no love for others. "What are you doing?" Jesus asked them plainly. "You're missing the point."

I don't want my kids to miss the point. I don't want them to have a religion; I want them to have a relationship. The things I adored about the church I grew up in simply point me back to Him—they are not the basis for my faith. They remind me of my faith, they support my faith, they are the aroma of my experiences that led to my faith, but they never were and never can be the sum total of my faith.

I don't want to pass old wineskins to my children (Matthew 9:17). I want to pass on a legacy of faith and a full understanding of the importance of being in community with others, loving on them, and being faithful in attendance even when they think they carry too much baggage.

What I really want for my kids is discipleship—the opportunity to rub shoulders and be mentored and disagree and grow and do the kind of 'one-anothering' Jesus demonstrated two thousand years ago.

So, I'm teaching them that going to church is more than just showing up and getting fed. It's doing life together. It's pursuing Jesus together. When I had our first baby, I did not cook a single meal for an entire month. We were still relative newcomers to our church, yet many of the meals, the prayers, and support came from this community of believers who recognized a young couple without family nearby who needed help. We stay fully plugged into that church to this day, not because they brought us food, but because there we hear the gospel and see it backed it up with transformed lives.

The heart and purpose of the Church is not about the music, the mission trips, the social justice or the next potluck. It very often includes those elements, but at its core, the purpose of church is to exalt God, edify believers, and evangelize the world, and to do it *together.*

If you've been hurt, insulted, let down, stereotyped, left out, misunderstood—welcome to the party. I'm not trying to be flippant or write off any pain you have endured by stepping foot into a community of believers, but I do know that whatever happened, it wasn't Jesus. If there's a measure of grace and forgiveness you need to extend, do it. And then, get yourself back there, even if it means laying down your pride. We can't expect fruit if we shortcut the growing process, and in a church setting that sometimes means sticking it out, showing up when you don't want to because ultimately, it's not about you.

So take the time to find the right community for you. It doesn't matter if it's in the woods or a run-down, gutted grocery store in the city, if it's in a home or an amphitheater or a cathedral. Find the people in pursuit of the fire and get among them. Do the hard, worthwhile work of living alongside people who, like you, are being transformed into the likeness of Christ.

CHAPTER FIFTEEN

CONTEND FOR JOY

Today the sky is Bahama blue and the kids are home for summer break, content with sticky banana popsicles and the sprinkler. The reality is far from idyllic, however. The air conditioner is fighting an uphill battle against the escalating heat of the day. A girlfriend calls and my phone is pressed against my sweaty cheek as I attempt to thinly slice zucchini with a dull kitchen knife. The slices are lopsided and chunky, my fingers nicked from the failed effort. The kids trail in from the yard, hungry and wet. *Someone poked someone. Someone might be bleeding. Where are the Band-Aids?*

A comedian once joked that having multiple kids is like trying to tread water and then someone hands you a baby. I've been treading in the deep end for a decade now, babies under each arm.

Parenthood has been more of a refining fire than any other life assignment I have been given, and I take it seriously; I feel the weight of this mission on my shoulders, in my bones, in the depths of my soul. Yet, I'm learning that joy has a way of lightening the load on this journey, not just making it bearable, but lifting the weight so we can all thrive.

I love being a mom, and if this is one of my greatest life assignments I don't just want to muddle through. I don't just want to survive it. I want to enjoy it. I want to thrive. When I get to the gates of Heaven and hear, "Well done, my good and faithful servant," I want much of that to be attributed to how I led these kids.

We read in Proverbs 14:1 that a wise woman builds her house, but what exactly does that mean for me? It means that Christ is the head of our marriage, Adam is the head of our household, and I am his partner, his helper, his collaborator, and his companion. I build our house by setting the atmosphere in our family. I spend most of my time with our kids, in our home, and I carry the most influence in that area.

A mother's place in the family is sacred and irreplaceable, and I don't want to do it with an unhappy heart or with a spirit that is not centered on Him. Ladies, do you know the incredible responsibility you have? You do not need to be rocked by the waves of your emotions or circumstances. Instead, you can create mindsets and habits that flow from Him until you have a home that your husband and kids want to be in. Not a perfect home, but a *joyful* home.

My friends tease me that I never yell. First off, that's not entirely true. I do yell, but it's not very often. It's not that I'm naturally calm or have mastered all the best ways to parent; it's that God has seriously pruned this area of my life during the past decade.

If there's a fire, I want to be the water and not the gasoline. Yes, it takes more self-control to stay calm, to exercise restraint, to pause and fashion whatever comes out of my mouth instead of yelling, but I have never regretted showing self-control. I have almost always regretted the yelling.

How are you bringing joy to your home? Are you purposefully creating an environment that reflects the tone Christ sets in our lives? Our libraries may be filled with parenting advice, but the best wisdom I can offer you is this: dive deep into the Word. When Jesus showed us what God is like, He showed us the Father. He modeled the perfect parenting relationship.

His Word is a reminder to come to Him daily and ask for His help. *I need Your cover, Your joy, Your steadfastness today in every little thing.* And there are a lot of little things when you have kids. I need wisdom about what spaces to sit in, what situations to move on from, what conversations to allow to roll, when to listen, when to speak with authority, or weave in advice or encouragement. If we ask, He gives freely.

Sometimes we come at motherhood full of bravado. *I got this. I got this.* And you might—at least for a little bit. But our momentum, our will, and our patience will eventually wax cold. You cannot get through motherhood on ambition alone. It's a marathon. The faster we lay down our pride, the faster we can get to the joy.

The book of Lamentations describes how God loves us—consistently, faithfully, unconditionally—and it's new for us every day, just like His joy: "The steadfast love of the Lord never ceases;

his mercies never come to an end; they are new every morning; great is your faithfulness" (Lamentations 3:22-23).

The Hebrew word for 'new' in this passage is *khadasha* or *chadash*; it means something fresh, or rebuilt, renewed, repaired. We like to trim the Lamentations verse and use it to remind each other simply that "His mercies are new every morning." It's short. It's sweet. It's refreshing. You can start again tomorrow. You can wake up and try again, have another shot. How can that not be encouraging?

Yes, His mercies *are* new every morning. The lessons are not. As a mother, I don't want to take advantage of that wide swathe of grace. I don't want to forsake the pruning or the guidance He gives me in this journey, because His intent is not to simply give me a free pass every day. His mercies are new each morning as I draw ever closer to Him.

It's heavy, yes. The stakes are high, yes. But don't let the challenges of this calling overshadow the joy. God calls the fruit of our wombs a heritage, a gift. Have you received that truth? Are you excited about that? Or are you wringing your hands over the details, all the things you are not doing right, all the things that could go wrong and do go wrong in a day?

We must contend for joy in motherhood in the same way we contend for our marriages, our careers, our health. I want to be intentionally joyful, and I want to build a home that is joyful despite our circumstances. It's possible, but only by continually seeking God's presence and realizing that His power is already within us (Colossians 1:29).

I want to do motherhood with intention—not just to discipline and correct my kids, but to intentionally *enjoy* them. The word 'enjoy' actually comes to us from the French—a derivative of *enjoir*—and means to make joy or to give joy. 'Enjoy' is a verb, an action, an exchange of emotion and energy between people. It's another one of God's masterful designs. He knew that within this sheath of motherhood, even with all its trials, that enjoying our children—actually delighting in them—would breathe life into our lungs.

Do you really enjoy your kids? Do you ever just stare at them and wonder, *how in the world are you even here?* I do—not in a creepy "I'm watching you" sort of way, but in a "I'm keenly aware that you are walking miracles, here to bring Him glory" kind of way.

What a fitting parallel to the creation story in Genesis. On the seventh day God stood back from His work and declared it good, satisfaction rolling over Him. He thought *we* were good. What a beautiful thought. We bring Him joy and our kids bring us the same.

Time continues to be the most precious commodity I have, and the closer we get to our kids not living in our home someday, I become more and more like a warrior, battling the distractions of the world to hold space with them, to have time together to notice all the little things. My oldest two have outgrown my lap. The hours and hours I spent rocking them to sleep at night, staring at their eyelashes and their plump fingers, wondering where they traveled in their dreams are all memories now.

In a few years we will have teenagers, and my friends tell me that's hard on a whole different level. Still, I hope there never comes a day I do not lay my burdens at His feet and continue to do the work of mothering with joy, whatever the season.

But for now, I want more time, more family dinners, more conversations. I don't want to panic if they tell me they're bored or if their whole day isn't curated with programs and activities and socialization. I don't want to come unglued if there's a snow day and we're all together, all day. I worried when friends told me that during the pandemic they couldn't handle being home all day, having that much time with their kids.

If God calls you to stay home, He'll give you exactly what you need each day, for each individual kid. Know that, just because you have hard days at home doesn't mean you shouldn't be there. I had challenging days at my job, and I have challenging days at home. The path of least resistance is not always the path you should be on. There will be moments of chaos and discord, moments of uncertainty, and that's okay. You will have spiritual battles at home because Satan will be after you—and because God will be pruning your heart. And you will exercise the spiritual muscles, discipline, habits and giftings God has given you in a way you could not anywhere else. What if, instead of running away from that, you ran toward it?

~

When you first carry a child, there's a moment of wonder when you realize that every molecule, every cell, every piece of DNA combined at exactly the right moment to create this being. Then even more miraculously, this baby grows and is born, then takes their first breath, then another, and then another.

This is God's kind of magic. He knows the number of hairs on my head at this very moment and how many will be whisked away by my brush tonight; He knows if somewhere deep inside me cancer cells are forming; He knows which joke I will laugh at tomorrow.

My mom said that she sat on the bed with my dad the day they brought me home from the hospital. Together they unswaddled me and just stared, awe washing over them. They counted all my toes, ran their fingers over my baby skin, peeked in my mouth, marveled at my hair. What a beautiful, profound thing—this discovering of our babies.

As our kids get older it's a different kind of discovery, like a butterfly unfurling its wings in front of you. You have to work a little harder to find out who they are becoming, what sin hides in the crevices of their heart, what makes them tick and ache and laugh. But the hints are everywhere, in the little things, like how fast anger bubbles to the surface, their rhythms of sleep, the passing comment about who they hope to be at twenty.

I listen to them talk, often as they munch on something in the kitchen or in the car. I'm witnessing the growth, the stretching and molding of their ideas and dreams. Sometimes it's silly and unfounded, unrealistic or wrong, and other times it's spot on, a revelation to me about how the world looks through their eyes.

Over summer we spend hours together at the lake, their backs long and lean, bending over buckets of minnows and perch. They are always on the hunt, in the stream or in the thick of the cattails, emerging with a toad or a tree frog clutched in their fingers. Our patio is overrun with buckets and plastic blue swimming pools of painted baby turtles, snakes, a snapping turtle.

My kids hug me often, and I worry someday they won't, so I keep them there as long as I can in my arms. With each hug it's like my chest is full of harp strings, taut and waiting, and as they put their little arms around my waist and a string is plucked, the reverberation moves all the way to my core.

I take pictures, way too many pictures, thousands of pictures. I realized by the time Elijah was two and I was pregnant with Brooke, that keeping them all organized and scrapbooked would be impossible. My mother-in-law bravely took on that mantle, and has sorted, cut, pasted and decorated oversized, colorful pages of photo albums, multiple books for each child. Someday they will take them to their own homes where they will be put on a shelf. Once a year, they will leaf through them and it will stir up the memories, like sweeping the broom around the corner of a dusty room, all the good and bad swirling around together.

On summer nights they linger in the back yard and plead for more time, and I acquiesce because the heat of the day has surrendered, the sun can't burn their shoulders anymore. The sky glows pale pink and peach and blue, and they drag blankets through the grass and up onto the black mat of the trampoline and wrap them around warm bodies, and they laugh. They just can't stop laughing, the kind of unbridled giddiness that creeps in at the end of a long day.

The stars appear in the sky, one at a time until we can't count them all. And if I stand at the far edge of the yard and tilt my head back long enough, my neck cramped, the expanse of the world above me overwhelms any question that lingers about who He is—for if the Maker can send these stars and place them with this precision, I can trust Him with these babies in the same way He trusts me with these babies. I am just a small part of a much greater thing.

~

I am most content, most unwound, when all four are at home in their beds. I dream some nights, and I see their freckled faces, bare feet, Hannah's red hair blowing in the wind, the echo of "Mom" calling out in each of their small voices.

Boy, girl, boy, girl. The boys have brown eyes, the girls blue. And together, in a pack, they are a force—a tangled, sweet, pulsating ball of energy, bouncing off each other but always coming back together like a rubber-band has been looped around them. And they fight, jockeying for control, to be first, to be the best. "One day," I tell them, "when mommy and daddy are gone . . ." They stop and listen, like I have said something foreign, something unspeakable. "Someday, it might just be the four of you, but you will have each other. You will always have each other."

I write a letter to each of them on their birthday: *This is who you are at two, at five, at eleven. This is why you have that scar on your lower lip, this is the year you wore the red hooded sweatshirt for days and days without washing it. You love green apples and hate green peppers, and you would drink milk, glass by glass, all day long if I let you. This is the year you fell in love with cheetahs. This is your gifting, your weaknesses, your nickname, and your one special spot in our family only you could occupy. Love you more deeply than you will ever know, Mommy.*

I hope that as they read these letters again someday they will act like a time capsule, a pulsating gift of the years that moved them through their childhood. I hope they see that we marked the time with purpose; we recognized it and didn't just let it pass us by. I hope the letters along with the albums accentuate and color the memories they carry in their hearts.

But until then, I am anchored to the present. My mom always tells me to write it down. "They said something funny, so write it down. You will forget." And she's right. The aroma of the present is strong and beautiful, then it disappears, and I can't get it back.

The memories accumulate, pearl after pearl after pearl on a long string winding its way back through the years. In my mind I can see the four of them picking through the thorns of a northern Michigan blackberry patch, spraying the slip-and-slide with olive oil, huddled around the Monopoly board, scooping snow into bowls to make homemade snow cones.

This was all part of His creation, His design. It is the weaving together of moments that lock your life into theirs, so when they do start to pull away—that natural process of them not needing you as much anymore, like a hot air balloon tethered to the earth, unlatching from its place and floating away on to its own path— letting go is not so hard. We love them with wild abandon. We hold nothing back. We do it with joy. And when the timing is right, they unfold and stretch and, filled with fire and warmth, lift off.

Last week our two eldest chose to be baptized, and when they emerged from the water I wrapped them in an oversized towel, kissed their wet heads, and felt my resolve to steward them well grow a little stronger. We celebrated the occasion—this public declaration of their beliefs—but I know it is just one of many steps in the building of their faith. Maybe that's the greatest lesson of sanctification, that it never ends. His water washes us clean, over and over and over. We look like Him a little more with every wash.

I declare God's promises over their lives, but I know this journey is not linear. They will struggle and bleed and hurt. My precious kids will walk through life with a yearning for Him, and the temptation will be to pursue something other than Him. Each day is an opportunity to say things that will settle deep into their bones, get stuck in their minds, imprint into their hearts, "You are loved, you are worthy, you are here for a purpose. And anything you try and do to replace that yearning for Him will leave you empty."

So, this is my promise to them: I will love you with reckless abandon. I will defend you. I will speak life over you. I will be a mama that prays deeply and fervently, until your last breath or mine, that you seek Him first.

And I refuse to do this with anything less than a whole heart—a heart that is completely sold out for Jesus and devoted to running this race in a way that honors Him. My race right now is steeped in motherhood, and I embrace that, I delight in it. It's not second best. It's not a cross I bear. It's pure joy.

He has placed in my hands these fragile, precious, strong-willed, barefoot beauties. And I'm so, so honored. I feel unworthy to be their mother in the same way I feel unworthy to be a vessel for Christ and His message—it's the greatest of callings, with the greatest of stakes.

Paul's second letter to the church at Corinth talks about this very thing: "If you only look at *us*, you might well miss the brightness. We carry this precious Message around in the unadorned clay pots of our ordinary lives. That's to prevent anyone from confusing God's incomparable power with us" (2 Corinthians 4:7 MSG). We are broken clay jars who have God's radiant, joy-filled light shining through the cracks. We are created, molded, precious moms filled with this one great purpose.

Isaiah 64:8 says, "We are the clay, and you are our potter; we are all the work of your hand." The idea that He chose to put greatness inside of me—this decaying, sinful, broken-down, prideful, vulnerable vessel—is deeply humbling.

This is what keeps me going as a Jesus-following mom—that bright, pulsing beat of hope that one day when I am not here and our four are grown, they will be living life in pursuit of His Kingdom, not distracted, not fearful, but *joyful.*

And maybe that day, when they are each stewarding their own littles, anchored in something bigger than themselves, they will look at each other and laugh about how they got here despite, or because of, the mismatched socks, that neighbor who used to yell at them, the late nights at the lake, the early Sunday mornings in the sanctuary, and so, so much more.

And I hope most of all, they say, "Yes, we had a mom who showed us Jesus. Our mom was full of radical joy."

ACKNOWLEDGMENTS

To my Mom and Dad. Thank you for loving me the way you do and always saving space for me to go where He calls. One of my greatest praises is that He chose me to be your daughter.

To my friends and family who doled out wisdom, inspired countless stories and offered their most precious commodity—their time: Tarrin Philpott, Alison Pindell, Leslee and Freddy Maseman, Katie Caldwell, Christi Hendrickson, Jolene Geary, Thomas and Alonna Fletcher, Jimmie Kammerer, Les and Sharon Potts, Lee and Liz Gahagan, Tesa Bryant, Anya Mueller, Meghan Renna, Cameron Stewart and McKenna Werbelow.

To that tribe of friends who taught me the blueprint for genuine discipleship and doing life together and continue to walk it out with me: Deanna McDaniel, Bobbi Jo Williams, Carisa Marshall and Kristen Kenner.

To the many friends and Bible study warriors who prayed, read drafts, filled in the gaps and consistently championed this project, thank you.

To my editor, Anya McKee, and the team at Torn Curtain Publishing: Thank you for believing in this book, praying over it, and for your wisdom, honesty and creativity.

To Joshua Doty and Olivia Viterna with Clokendagger, and to Megan Merscheim. Thank you for catching this vision and running with it.

To Ben and Havilah Cunnington, Michelle-Wade Raftery, Vikki Waters, Morgan Williams, Havilah's Author School staff, and my fellow writing coaches. Thank you for praying, for lighting the fire to finish, and finally, providing the guard rails to get to the end. You said I would write this book, but in the end, it would write me. You were right. God is so good, and I'm grateful.

CPSIA information can be obtained
at www.ICGtesting.com
Printed in the USA
JSHW011029150623
43193JS00001B/7